Thomas Nettleship Staley

Five Years' Church Work in the Kingdom of Hawaii

Thomas Nettleship Staley

Five Years' Church Work in the Kingdom of Hawaii

ISBN/EAN: 9783337138172

Printed in Europe, USA, Canada, Australia, Japan

Cover: Foto ©ninafisch / pixelio.de

More available books at **www.hansebooks.com**

IVE YEARS' CHURCH WORK IN THE KINGDOM OF HAWAII

BY THE BISHOP OF HONOLULU

RIVINGTONS

London, Oxford, and Cambridge

1868

Preface

I AM so frequently asked for information as to the circumstances in which the Mission of the Church of England to the Sandwich Islands originated, and for particulars regarding its progress and work, that I thought it well to embody the elements of what might be said on these subjects in the present volume.

In doing so, I have chosen to compile from documents before me, rather than assert facts merely on my own authority; and to abstain, as much as possible, from drawing from those facts conclusions which the reader is competent to draw for himself.

Nor is it my aim in so narrow a compass to give an exhaustive view even of the religious, much less of the general social condition of the Hawaiian kingdom. Any one who wishes to inform himself further on these subjects may peruse the delightful and instructive work of Mr. Manley Hopkins, entitled "Hawaii, Past and Present."

If those who have aided the cause of the Anglican branch of Christ's Holy Catholic Church in these Islands of the Pacific are convinced by what they here read, that their efforts for the moral and spiritual good of an interesting and noble race have not been wholly in vain, it will amply justify the present publication.

T. N. H.

Contents

	PAGE
I. "COME OVER AND HELP US"	1
II. RESPONSE TO THE CALL	13
III. THE FIRST YEAR	22
IV. TWO MONTHS OF SORROW	30
V. POSITION OF THE CHURCH SINCE THE DEATH OF KAMEHAMEHA IV.—ITS WORK	51
VI. DIFFICULTIES AND PROSPECTS	83
VII. SKETCH OF THE ISLANDS AND PEOPLE, COMMERCE, SOCIAL CONDITION, ETC.	96
APPENDIX	110
ADDENDA	125

List of Illustrations

PORTRAITS OF THE KAMEHAMEHAS	to face title-page.	
MAP	to face page	1
MEMORIAL CHURCH AND CATHEDRAL OF S. ANDREW, HONOLULU	,,	13
PORTRAIT OF THE PRINCE OF HAWAII	,,	20
LAHAINA (MAUI)	,,	29
ROYAL MAUSOLEUM, HONOLULU	,,	37
S. ALBAN'S COLLEGE FOR BOYS, NUUANU VALLEY, HONOLULU	,,	54
S. ANDREW'S PRIORY, HONOLULU, FOR THE SISTERHOOD AND GIRLS' BOARDING-SCHOOL	,,	58
HOSPITAL OF S. CROSS, FOR THE SISTERHOOD AND INDUSTRIAL GIRLS' SCHOOL, LAHAINA	,,	60
KEALAKEKUA BAY, KONA		66
CLERGY-HOUSE AND SCHOOL-CHURCH, WAILUKU MAUI		76

FIVE YEARS' CHURCH WORK,

&c.

I.

"COME OVER AND HELP US."

THE circumstances connected with the discovery of the Hawaiian Archipelago by Captain Cook are too well known to need repetition. Twelve years later, we find Captain Vancouver visited the group (1792—1794). At that time the leading chieftain of the large island of Hawaii was Kamehameha, the Great, as the natives call him, the founder of the dynasty which has since borne his name. With him Vancouver had frequent interviews, using as interpreters two Englishmen, John Young[1] and Isaac Davis, then living at his court. These men had been taken

---

[1] John Young married a native woman of rank, through whom their granddaughter, the good Queen Emma, traces her lineage to the ancient royal stock of Hawaii.

prisoners in the year 1786 by Kamehameha, in revenge for a massacre, which the crew of an American vessel had wantonly perpetrated on a party of natives assembled on the beach. They were treated kindly by the chieftain, rose to be chiefs themselves, and gained much influence over him—an influence, to their credit be it said, ever exerted on the side of humanity and civilization. Vancouver imported horses, sheep, cattle, and other things which the islands most needed, and sought to encourage trade and the pursuits of peace. He told Kamehameha, too, "of the one true God, the Creator and Ruler of the Universe," and promised on his return to England to request King George to send him a " teacher of the true religion[2]."

Vancouver seems to have remembered his promise, for, when in England, he sought to impress on Mr. Pitt the duty of sending missionaries to the islands. But it was a time when the minds of men were taken up with the events then transpiring on the Continent; neither was it a missionary age, and a great opportunity was lost to our Church.

From the period of Vancouver's departure, the King of Hawaii was principally occupied in reducing the

[2] See Jarves's "History of the Sandwich Islands" (Honolulu, 1847), p. 88.

eight islands under his own undivided sway, in consolidating his power, and establishing something like order and law in his dominions. He carried on a considerable trade with the vessels touching there. White settlers usually received a kind welcome, and grants of land [3]. There can be no doubt that a growing intercourse with civilized life, unfavourable as might be sometimes the specimens of it presented to his view, had the effect of shaking old beliefs, and infusing into the minds of the people a spirit of discontent with their heathen rites and oppressive *tabu*. The changes, too, which had occurred in Tahiti, in the final triumph of Christianity there through the labours of the London Missionary Society, had, it is said, also an influence during the last few years of Kamehameha's reign, in exciting within him a spirit of inquiry and a desire to learn more of that Supreme Being whom the foreigners professed to worship. "Unfortunately, the whites around him were little able, even had they been disposed, to explain the sub-

[3] The Rev. J. Williamson, S. P. G. Missionary, Kona, Hawaii, writes, under date Sept. 9, 1867, of one of these early settlers: "Old Mr. P—— is on his death-bed. Hearing of this, I rode over to see him. He was very thankful. I regret the distance hinders me from visiting him regularly. He lives on the mountain, seventy miles off. Mr. P—— is one of the oldest foreign residents, having come in 1809."

lime truths, or tell him of the heavenly tidings of the Gospel; and on the 8th of May, 1819, he died, as he had lived, in the faith of his country[4]."

His son Liholiho succeeded him, and soon gave evidence of the little faith which he felt in the existing religious system. The prevalent scepticism found in him a willing exponent. The word went forth, the idols were abolished by edict, the "taboo" was broken, the Heiaus (sacred enclosures serving as their temples) were thrown down, their ruins being still visible in several spots on the islands.

In this remarkable movement the high priest, Hewahewa, himself took the lead. It was the following year that the first missionaries arrived, and found the way wonderfully opened by this revolution for a favourable reception of their message[5]. They were Presbyterians and Congregationalists, from New England. The promise of Vancouver, however, to endeavour to send *English* missionaries had not been forgotten, though a quarter of a century had passed by since it was given; and, consequently, some little hesitation seems to have been felt by the chiefs about permitting these first messengers of the Cross to

[4] Jarves's History, p. 105.
[5] See "Missionary Register" (1821).

establish their mission. Mr. Young was ordered to write to this country, and inform its rulers that, "American teachers had come to labour among the people."

The arrival of Messrs. Tyerman and Bennett (of the London Missionary Society) in 1822, and of the Rev. W. (now Dr.) Ellis, then a missionary at Tahiti, proved of much use in removing the suspicions with which at first the objects of these earnest men were regarded. The language was put into a written shape, a task of no little difficulty. Ere long, the New Testament and, some time later, the whole Bible were translated into Hawaiian. In these respects we, who are called to "labour in the Vineyard" at this more advanced stage in the history of the Hawaiian kingdom, may truly say, "Other men have laboured, and we are entered into their labours."

The King, the leading chiefs and chiefesses, eagerly engaged in the task of learning to read. Books were printed, of course of a very rudimentary kind; and among scholars so apt as the Hawaiians naturally are, it is no marvel that at least the elements of knowledge were acquired.

In 1823 Liholiho (Kamehameha II.) and his Queen embarked for England, having resolved to incur the risks of a long and tedious voyage, in the hope, it is said, of placing their kingdom under the protection of the British Crown. (They had, however, other aims.) In acknowledging the gift of a schooner sent out by the British Government for his use, the King, in a letter to George IV. (Aug. 21, 1822), had remarked, "Our former idolatrous system has been abolished, as we wish the Protestant religion of *your Majesty's dominions* to be practised here." And we have the authority of his late Majesty Kamehameha, in the Preface to the Hawaiian Book of Common Prayer, for believing that the realization of this wish was one of the reasons why the long voyage was undertaken [6].

The expedition, however, had a very unfortunate end. Liholiho and his Queen died in London. Their remains were sent back to the islands, with all due honours, in a British man-of-war, "La Blonde," Captain Lord Byron [7]. Kekuanoa, the present King's father, who had accompanied the party to England, while

---

[6] "Ua kauohaia aku o Vanekopa e hoouna mai i ke Akua oiaio. Ua kii aku o Iolani i ka aina e, e lawe ia mai." "Vancouver was asked to send us the knowledge of the true God. Iolani visited foreign lands to obtain it."

[7] Late Admiral Lord Byron, who died at Brighton early in the present year (1868).

returning home in this vessel, was baptized by the chaplain on board. He is still living, and at the time of the arrival of the English mission in 1862 was Governor of the Island of Oahu, and President of the Board of Education. As the first baptized member of the Church, he was nominated by his late Majesty, with other leading persons in the islands, as one of its lay representatives; and his name stands as such in the charter of incorporation granted in 1862. This was done in anticipation of his expected confirmation, and of his becoming a communicant. But the influence of his early training, and his thirty years' connexion with the Congregational body, has prevented his taking any active part in establishing the Church invited by his lamented son, or in attending but very rarely its ministrations.

Kauikeaouli became King on the death of his brother Liholiho, with the title of Kamehameha III.; but being a minor, Kaahumanu, one of the wives of Kamehameha I., acted as regent. It was not till 1829 that the young King began to take any active part in the administration of the government. Attempts were now made to introduce the Roman Church into the Islands; but, owing to the opposition of the chiefs, acting under the inspiration of the Congregational mission, without success. The priests who first landed were banished, and their converts subjected to severe penalties. It was not till 1839, on the visit of the French frigate "L'Artémise," Captain Laplace, that permission was granted the Roman missionaries to commence their labours. The following were among the demands enforced on the Hawaiian Government: "(1) The free toleration of the Roman Catholic faith. (2) The release of all persons suffering imprisonment for professing its tenets. (3) A deposit of 20,000 dollars in the hands of the captain, as a guarantee for the future. (4) That a site should be granted in fee-simple for the erection of a church in Honolulu." There was no other course but to yield to these peremptory conditions; and from that time to the present the Roman Catholic Church has enjoyed in the islands a free toleration, numbering at this time one-third of the population within its fold.

In 1840 a sort of Constitution was proclaimed, under which the government was confided, under the King, to a council of chiefs. The Congregationalist missionaries at this time wielded, and continued to do so for some years, the greatest influence in the administration; and in 1852 the King was induced to grant a still further concession to Democracy in the shape of a Constitution based on "universal suffrage, vote by ballot, paid members, no property qualification." Kauikeaouli seems to have had some misgivings as to the expediency of this measure, or at least to have felt that it was an experiment; for when he gave his consent, he made the remark, that "the same power which granted the Constitution could take it away." All traces of feudal rights disappeared from the statute-book, so to say, though not from the social system of the country.

Meanwhile the business of the Islands was increasing. In 1846 no less than 674 vessels touched at the ports, far the greater part engaged in the whaling trade of the Pacific. The effect of such an intercourse between the natives and some of the worst specimens of our own race was painfully manifested in the spread of vice and disease, and the rapid diminution of the people. Foreign residents, however, increased in number. The year 1845 is memorable for the arrival at Honolulu of Mr. Robert Crichton Wyllie, a Scotch gentleman of fortune, who was ere long placed by the King in the responsible office of Foreign Minister, which he continued to hold for nearly twenty-five years. To his zeal, industry, loyalty, and devotion to the interests of the kingdom, is due in no small degree the fact that Hawaii now holds a place in the family of recognized nations.

In 1847 the Princes Alexander Liholiho and Lot Kamehameha, children of Kinau, the then King's sister, by Kekuanoa, were sent on a voyage to the United States, England, and France. They had been carefully instructed from boyhood in the English language; hence that great superiority in general intelligence and cultivation which distinguished them from the mass of their fellow-countrymen. These young Princes met with kindly notice at our own court as well as elsewhere. They made a very favourable impression, and gathered new ideas, which were not lost upon them as regarded both the English State and the English Church. At Westminster Abbey they attended Divine Service, with the beauty and solemnity of which they were much struck. The writer has been permitted to hear read portions of the diary which the late King, then Prince Liholiho, kept during his stay in England. It records the sights and events of each day, with the impressions that they left upon this young chief's mind, written in excellent English and in good taste.

In 1855 Kamehameha III. (Kauikeaouli) died, and was succeeded by his nephew, Alexander Liholiho Iolani, with the title of Kamehameha the Fourth. Soon after his accession, the young King married Emma, granddaughter of John Young (of whom mention has been already made), and the adopted child of T. C. Rooke, Esq., M.D., a leading foreign resident at Honolulu. Dr. Rooke had given her the advantage of being taught by an English governess, a lady who is still living in the Islands. The nuptials were celebrated by one of the Congregationalist missionaries, but, at the request of the King, according to the Marriage Service of the Book of Common Prayer.

The rejoicing was great when it was announced that a son and heir to the crown had been born to the royal pair. As the child grew, he became the idol of the people. His mother taught him herself his morning and evening prayers, and the first principles of the Christian faith. It was the King's great ambition to have him sent, when old enough, to one of the great public schools in England, but in the interval some suitable provision had to be made for educating the Prince of Hawaii at home. With this consideration, others combined to suggest to the King the advantages which would result from the presence of a branch of the Church of England in Hawaii. Often had he spoken in public of the want of *industrial female boarding-schools*, where the future wives and mothers of the land might be trained in the principles of morality and religion[8]. At Honolulu were some hundreds of British and American residents eager to welcome the Church of their baptism. Lastly, the licentiousness and heathenism, still widely prevalent according to the testimony of the American missionaries themselves[9], might be expected to receive no slight check by the introduction of a new Christian influence enjoying the thorough sympathy of the rulers of the people.

[8] "Collected Speeches of King Kamehameha IV." (Honolulu).
[9] "Report of Hawaiian Evangelical Association for 1863," *passim*.

II.

RESPONSE TO THE CALL.

IT was early in the year 1861 that the Bishop of Oxford, in a discussion which took place in the Upper House of Convocation, on the subject of Missionary Bishoprics, spoke as follows :—

" That the King of the Sandwich Islands was most anxious to see a Bishop of the English Church established in his dominions. His Majesty mentioned that, ' according to the Constitution of his kingdom, no established Church, in the proper sense of the term, can be formed there ; that all creeds are left free, to be supported by voluntary contributions.' He proposes to make the Bishop preceptor to the Crown Prince. He thought it best to communicate with the Queen, and wrote a letter, in most excellent English, begging Her Majesty to give all the assistance she could in sending out a Bishop of the Church of which she is the temporal head. The present mail has brought me a letter from the Bishop of California, who points out the importance of making the islands a missionary centre. Further, the American Church is very anxious to unite with the Church of England in this work[1]. And Bishop Potter states that they will undertake to support one or possibly two Missionary Clergy, to work with the Bishop whom the Church of England may send out. All this is matter of the deepest interest and the greatest importance; and I think it most important that we should at once consider the question. If God opens to us new fields, we ought to turn our attention to them, and to occupy them in a manner consistently with primitive customs and primitive practice, and to follow out historical precedents in extending the Kingdom of Christ."

The invitation of the King to our Church being thus publicly and formally announced, and the difficulty to its acceptance being the need of funds, the course usual under such circumstances was taken. Those who sympathized with the object came together and formed a committee, consisting of Church dignitaries, noblemen, and gentlemen; several of them members of the committees of the two venerable

---

[1] See in Appendix, Letter from Right Rev. Dr. Kip to the "Pacific Churchman" (1866).

Societies for the Propagation of the Gospel in Foreign Parts, and for the Promotion of Christian Knowledge.

Within one month after the Bishop of Oxford's speech in Convocation, the following statement was published and circulated:—

"POLYNESIAN CHURCH.—The committee for promoting the establishment of a Church in Honolulu, in communion with the Churches of England and America, having taken into consideration the King of Hawaii's desire to receive a mission from the Church of England headed by a Bishop, are of opinion that measures should be taken for fulfilling the desire thus put, we trust, by God into the heart of His Majesty.

"That having respect to the importance of these Islands as a probable centre of Christian influence in the North Pacific Archipelago, as well as to the immediate needs of the actual population of the Hawaiian group, an earnest appeal for support be made to the Church at home.

"That as it appears by letters from the Bishops of California and New York, that there is a readiness on behalf of the American Church to unite in this effort, the committee hail with gratitude to God such an opening for common missionary action between the two great branches of the Reformed Catholic Church.

"That the Bishops of California and New York be requested to convey to the Church in America most earnest invitations from this committee to unite in the work.

"The city of Honolulu contains, besides its native population, European and American residents. The French Roman Catholics possess a cathedral, with a Bishop, clergy, &c., and the American Congregationalists have also places of worship. The King offers on his own behalf and that of his subjects and residents who desire the establishment of the English Church, a yearly payment of 200*l.* and to give the site for a church, parsonage, &c. It is also probable that a grant of land may be made for the future support of the Mission. The resources of the Islands can probably not do much more at present than this, and the committee appeal with earnestness to their fellow Churchmen to assist in sending forth labourers into this part of the Lord's vineyard."

The two venerable Societies, the Society for the

Propagation of the Gospel, and the Society for Promoting Christian Knowledge, immediately signified their approval of the movement by liberal grants in its aid.

After some discussion as to the manner in which the consecration of a Missionary Bishop should be performed, whether or not with any action on the part of the Crown, it was finally decided that the Royal Licence was necessary. And on the 15th of December, the consecration of an English Bishop for the newly-created see of Honolulu took place in Lambeth Chapel, by the then Primate, Archbishop Sumner, assisted by the Bishops of London and Oxford.

It was the morning when England awoke to learn how vast a loss she had sustained in the death of the Prince Consort, and when every nerve of the country was quivering under the blow!

A farewell service for the Mission party was held in Westminster Abbey, when the Bishop preached, and the Holy Communion was administered to a large number, chiefly the friends and supporters of the undertaking. The celebrant was the Dean, the present Archbishop of Dublin, assisted by the Bishops of Oxford and Capetown. A few days before the departure of the Bishop from England, he received from the Archbishop of Canterbury the following letter :—

"My dear Bishop,—

"I am much gratified by your kind note, and the opportunity which it gives me of wishing you farewell, which my state of health has prevented my being able to do, as I could have wished, in person.

"I have also to thank you for the sermon which you have forwarded to me, and the assurance which I receive from it (not that I wanted it before) that the blessing of the Head of the Church will accompany your ministry.

"My earnest prayers go with you and your family, devoting yourselves, as you have done, to a work which few would have undertaken. I shall not survive to hear of the success granted you; but what we know not now, we shall know hereafter.

"T. B. Cantuar."

These words of sympathy and encouragement were among the last written by the venerable Primate.

The Mission party, consisting of the Bishop of Honolulu and family, the Rev. G. Mason, M.A., and the Rev. E. Ibbotson, embarked at Southampton for the Isthmus of Panama, on the 17th of August, 1862. By the kind permission of the Rev. Mark Cooper, Vicar, the Holy Communion was celebrated in St. Mary's Church at 8 a.m. (specially for the Mission), notice having been given to that effect in all the churches of the town the day before, which happened to be Sunday. The communicants numbered nearly 100, and the offertory was devoted to the fund of the Hawaiian Church.

The first part of the voyage terminated at Colon, or, as the Americans call it, Aspinwall, the port on the Atlantic side of the Isthmus of Panama. Here services were held on Sunday, September 7th, in a Wesleyan chapel, kindly placed by its minister at the disposal of the Bishop; and several persons were publicly confirmed. The seed thus sown was not without yielding its fruit; for a neat Gothic church has been since erected by the Panama Railroad Company at this place, in connexion with the Episcopal Church of the United States.

It ought here to be mentioned that the managers of this American line, with praiseworthy liberality, remitted the usual charge for excess of baggage, on the ground of its belonging to missionaries; thereby saving the party upwards of 50*l.* sterling—an example which our English companies might well imitate.

On the 10th of September, the Bishop and party sailed from Panama, the old Spanish city on the Pacific side of the Isthmus, and arrived in San Francisco after a voyage of fourteen days. Here they were kindly received by the Bishop of California, Dr. Kip, and the American clergy of the city. A vessel was on the eve of sailing for Honolulu, in which, after a rest of two days, they embarked.

The weather was propitious. On the twelfth day of the voyage Molokai and Mani were passed, looking beautiful in the setting sun. In the morning the vessel was off Honolulu. Full of thankfulness and hope, the Bishop and his companions held their last service in their little barque. Scarce had they risen from their knees, than they were greeted with the sad tidings, brought on board by the pilot, "The Prince of Hawaii is dead!"

Every member of the Mission felt this as an almost fatal blow. The baptism of the Prince had been anticipated as the inauguration, so to say, of the work. Her Majesty Queen Victoria had graciously consented to stand sponsor at the ceremony; and she had sent out by the hands of the newly-arrived

THE PRINCE OF HAWAII

British representative, Mr. W. W. F. Synge, an appropriate gift for her god-child, while Mrs. Synge was to act as her proxy. It was found on inquiry, that a Congregational minister had been summoned to baptize the little fellow privately, his distracted parents having first sent to the British man-of-war, "Termagant," which had lately arrived in port, to see if there were a chaplain on board. Alas! there was none.

III.

THE FIRST YEAR.

NO sooner had the vessel anchored, than Mr. Wyllie, the Foreign Minister, and Mr. Gregg, Minister of Finance, an American, came on board to receive the Mission in the King's name. They were followed by a deputation of the Church Committee and other residents. The royal carriage was placed at the disposal of the Bishop, and every thing done to show him respect and welcome. It happened to be Saturday; but by the next day a building, formerly used as a Wesleyan chapel, had been arranged for Divine service. After an early communion, English matins were celebrated at eleven o'clock, when there was a full congregation, consisting chiefly of foreign residents, Hawaiians filling up all the vacant space, and thronging round the doors and windows. An eloquent and impressive sermon was preached by Mr. Mason. The King and Queen arrived at the palace the following week from the country, whither they had retired in the first outburst of their grief. Both were deeply moved when the Bishop was introduced to them by Mr. Wyllie. After a few touching words referring to his recent loss, yet bidding us a hearty welcome to the Islands, the King said he had already completed his translation of the Morning and Evening Prayers and Litany into the Hawaiian language, and that it was then in the hands of the printer. He recommended the immediate enlargement of the temporary church, which was accordingly at once undertaken. An aisle in wood was added. The building, as a whole, was made more suitable for the ritual of the English Church. The royal seat was draped in black; and immediately over the entrance was an illuminated legend, "If we suffer, we shall also reign with Him." The inaugural sermon of the Mission was preached on October 19th by the Bishop, in English, before the King, Queen, and leading residents. On October 23rd a meeting was held in the court-house of those who desired to attend the ministrations of the Church, the Attorney-General, Mr. Harris, a member of the American branch of the Church, presiding. The King was present. Resolutions were carried, welcoming the English Mission, and pledging annual contributions towards its support. It was determined at once to apply to the Government for a Charter of Incorporation, which was granted. The Bishop, the clergy in priests' orders, and certain laymen nominated by the King, were to be trustees of all such funds as might be obtained from local sources or sent to them through the hands of the Bishop, from England and America. By the terms of the Charter, the voice of the laity is limited to matters of a purely secular kind. Provision was made for the permanence of the corporation by a clause requiring each congregation to elect some communicant member as a laydelegate to represent them. A Finance Committee, with a layman to act as treasurer, was also appointed.

On October 21st Queen Emma was baptized in the palace, in the presence of all the leading chiefs and foreign residents in the kingdom. On November 9th the first Hawaiian service was celebrated, consisting of matins and sermon. The latter was, of course, a written one, and it had been submitted to the King before its delivery. His Majesty corrected the translation where it was defective, and then heard it read over by the preacher several times till the pronunciation was deemed satisfactory. During the greater part of the following year it was his wont every week to render this invaluable service to the Bishop or the clergy. The delight of the natives was unbounded when they joined, for the first time in their own language, in the grand and solemn offices of our Liturgy.

For some weeks their Majesties were under preparation and instruction for the Holy Rite of Confimation. The day fixed for it was November the 28th, which happened to be a public holiday, kept in commemoration of the recognition of the national independence of England and France. The following is a description of this memorable incident, by one of the clergy, in a letter to friends in England :—

"The hour fixed for the ceremony was 10.30, but long before that time the temporary cathedral was besieged by hundreds anxious to gain admittance. One-third of the church was reserved for members of the Court, House of Nobles, and Consular body; another for the regular congregation, and the rest for the native population. The street was occupied by His Majesty's troops—viz., the cavalry, infantry, and rifle volunteers. Precisely at 10.30 the procession entered the church, consisting of the choir of native boys and men vested in surplices, and the

Bishop and clergy. At the same moment the sounds of the National Anthem announced the approach of their Majesties; and the Bishop, attended by his chaplain, the Rev. G. Mason, received the King and Queen at the west door. Here the King and Queen knelt down, having begged the Bishop to give them his blessing. His Lordship immediately pronounced Episcopal benediction, and then conducted their Majesties to their seats. The service commenced with the Litany, chanted in Hawaiian, the choir responding in harmony; from the musical nature of the language, it had a most solemn and beautiful effect, and the harmony of the responses was perfect. The Litany ended, we then left the church for the vestry, where we re-formed in the following order:—Major Kaauwai (the King's aide-de-camp), vested in surplice, and carrying the Bishop's banner; choristers (native boys and men, two and two), clergy, chaplain bearing pastoral staff, and the Bishop. The procession left the vestry and entered the church at the west door, chanting the 19th Psalm, to the 3rd tone, 2nd ending. Their Majesties then left their seats, and stood in front of the altar. The address was read by the Rev. G. Mason. The Bishop having put the question, their Majesties replied in a clear, audible voice. All kneeling, the Bishop said the prayers. His Lordship then called upon the congregation to spend a few moments in silent prayer on behalf of those to be confirmed. The request was responded to in earnest. Those few moments were indeed silent and solemn; the congregation then rose and sang the *Veni Creator* over their Majesties, who remained kneeling. We sang it to the ancient Gregorian melody. The Bishop then confirmed the King and Queen, and afterwards delivered an impressive address. Their Majesties were deeply affected, and so were the people, judging from their devout behaviour and attention. The natives especially seemed to enter into every thing; and many shed tears of joy and thankfulness when they saw their beloved Sovereign and his consort kneeling before the altar, and under the consecrated hands of their Bishop. One elderly chief remarked to his son, after service, that 'if a man did not know English, or even if he were quite deaf, still he might understand all that was passing before him from what he *saw*.' Before the Blessing we sang the 100th Psalm. After the service was over, the King and Queen returned to the Palace, the band playing as before, the guns firing a royal salute. The altar was vested in white, and decorated with flowers, offered by members of the congregation. The King wore his uniform, which is similar to that of an English field-marshal; the Queen was dressed in white, and wore a long white veil. We said Evensong, as usual, at 7.30, and Friday happening to be the evening for the Hawaiian service, the church was crowded with natives; after which we sang a *Te Deum* in the native language as the closing act of this happy and important day. May it be blessed to their Majesties as well as to their country! will ever be the prayer of us all; and I think our kind friends at home will join in this intercession. Three of the King's officers have also been confirmed—viz., his Excellency the Hon. R. C. Wyllie, Prime Minister; the Hon. G. M. Robertson, Vice-Chancellor; and the Attorney-General, C. C. Harris, Esq. On Advent Sunday the King and Queen, with the above-mentioned, made their first Communion."

The year which followed the royal Confirmations was one of steady, silent progress in Church-work. Mrs. Mason began a female boarding-school at Honolulu, the King being at an expense of about 4000 dollars in the erection of suitable buildings for

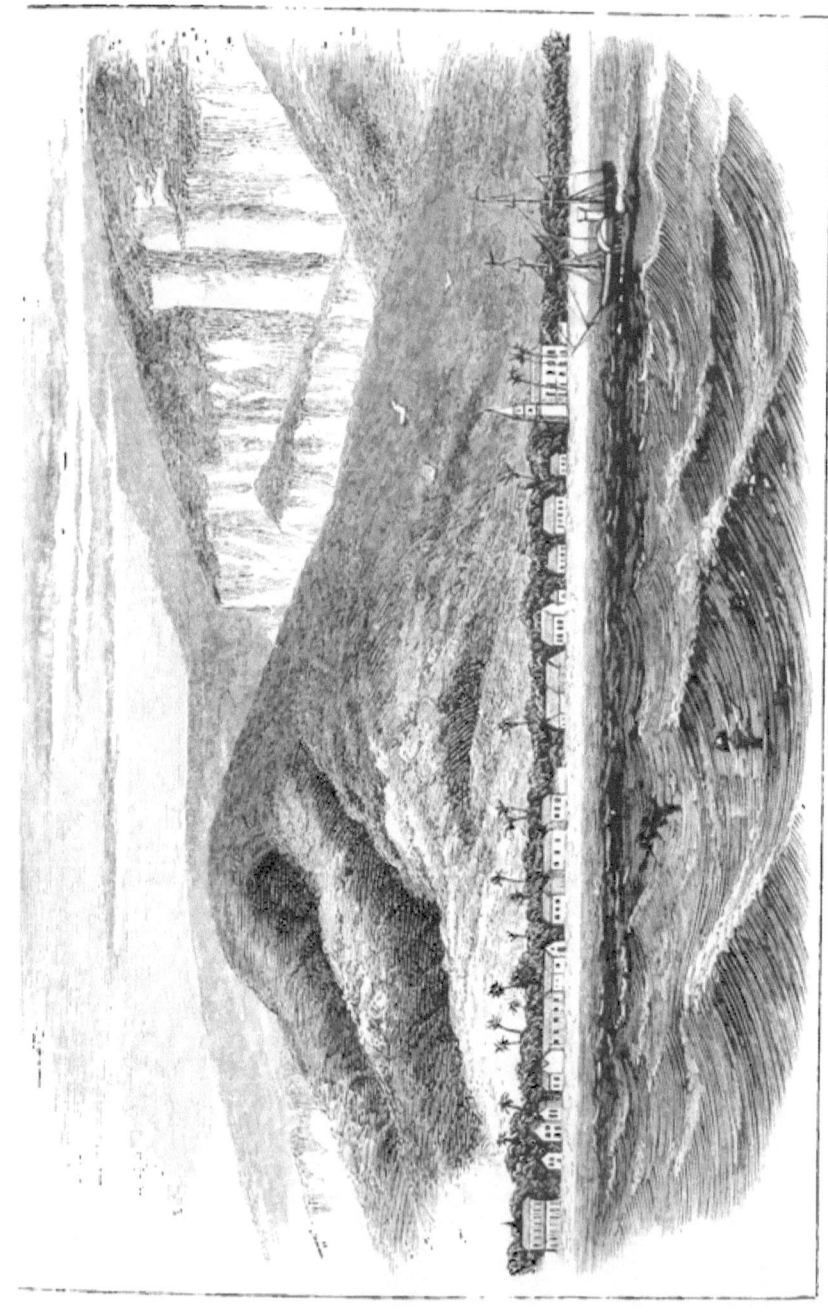

LAHAINA (MAUI)

this institution. A district visiting society was established, of which Queen Emma and other ladies, native and foreign, became working members. A guild of Hawaiian communicants was formed, " to make known the principles of the Church, as distinguished from Popery and Calvinism, to distribute tracts, teach in the Sunday-schools, read parts of the King's Prayer Book in small gatherings of people, and look out persons for confirmation." Early in 1863 a second station was opened at Lahaina, in the island of Maui, with a meeting held in the Courthouse, at which resolutions, welcoming the Bishop and his coadjutors, were moved by the Governor and other chiefs, and carried by acclamation. Often were the King and Queen seen standing side by side at the font, to answer for the little ones whom they brought to receive Holy Baptism, and for whose proper training and instruction they made themselves responsible. Unions long unblest of Heaven were, through their instrumentality, now sealed in holy matrimony, " in the sight of God and His Church." Such was the work going on in Honolulu and Lahaina, when another severe loss befell the Mission, in the untimely and sudden death of its founder and friend, King Kamehameha IV., on St. Andrew's day, 1863.

IV.

TWO MONTHS OF SORROW.

THE particulars of this sad event were described at the time in a letter from the Bishop, printed in the "Guardian" newspaper of Feb. 17, 1864. The following is an extract:—

"His Majesty had been for some time in a weak state of health, but no danger was apprehended till an hour before his decease. For several days he had suffered from diarrhœa, and was greatly reduced. When his state was pronounced by his medical attendants to be critical, I was summoned by the Queen, but arrived a few minutes too late. His old and faithful Foreign Minister, Mr. Wyllie, was however present, and in my absence read the Commendatory Prayer. His Majesty expired in the arms of his loving consort at 9 a.m. When I entered the room, she was fondly endeavouring to restore animation by breathing into his mouth her own warm breath. It was indeed a touching sight. When she saw all her efforts were of no avail, she begged me to pray. Most of the members of the Royal Family were present, and we all knelt down and implored our Heavenly Father to grant us resignation to His will, and strength to endure with meekness the sudden and unexpected chastisement. We were all overwhelmed with grief. The body lay in state the following day, Tuesday, the 1st of December. Between 3000 and 4000 people, residents and Hawaiians, passed through the throne-room to take a last fond look at their beloved Sovereign. The wailing of the natives was truly piteous and must have been heard far and near.

"The funeral will not take place for a month. A new royal cemetery is being prepared, which I am to consecrate; and it is the national custom to give every one the opportunity, even if they have to come from the remote islands, of visiting the remains of a deceased Sovereign before they are interred. Meanwhile the Queen sits almost incessantly by the coffin. She has prayers in the room night and morning, in the Hawaiian language, so that all present may understand, taken from the Book of Common Prayer; and

I read to her from the Psalms or other consolatory passages of Holy Scripture every day. It is beautiful to see how she seeks for consolation only in God. Twice since her bereavement I have administered to her the Holy Communion. Among all classes of people there is one common feeling of sympathy with her in this hour of her anguish. For by her works of charity and mercy, she had endeared herself to the hearts of all. The late King had received the Holy Communion on Sunday, Nov. 15, two weeks before his death. That day he was too unwell to be at church. He requested me, therefore, to celebrate in the Palace with him and the Queen. On Sunday the 22nd he was at the native Litany at 6.30 p.m., and I was struck with the earnest and devout manner in which he joined in the responses. This was the last time he was at church. No one loved our services more devotedly or attended them more regularly. Often he would be present at the early six o'clock celebrations. Let me give a proof of his correct views with regard to the Holy Eucharist, as the highest act of Christian worship. Two months ago, he and the Queen were thrown out of their carriage. They escaped with a few bruises and sprained ankles. The King sent for me the next morning at six o'clock to give him the Holy Communion; 'for,' he said, 'when we have received signal mercies, there is no higher form by which we can express our gratitude than the 'sacrifice of praise and thanksgiving.' At 7.30 o'clock on Sunday mornings before his last indisposition, he used to breakfast with his dependants in the verandah of the Palace, and conclude always with prayers selected from the Hawaiian Liturgy. The death of his only son, the little Prince of Hawaii, who was to have been educated by us, gave a shock to his system from which he never recovered. There can be no doubt from thenceforth he was a broken-hearted man. But he sought comfort in furthering the work of the Church he loved so much, and in translating the Book of Common Prayer. He saw in its wide diffusion through the Islands the great spiritual instrument for raising his subjects to a higher moral life. I might name many instances of his devotion and zeal in the cause he had embraced; but this may suffice.

"The Sunday following his decease, the church was crowded at all the services. The Ministers and Court attended at the Hawaiian service, and I preached on the occasion. The sermon has been printed in the native newspaper. The church was almost lined with black; the altar-cloth and reredos in deep mourning (this was done at the expense of the Legislature). Two large *Kahilis*[2], the symbols of royal authority, and the King's military hat and sword, were placed conspicuously in the royal pew. A beautiful lament in Hawaiian was sung by the choir, to the air, 'Can those eyes in death reposing.' All was most touching and solemn. We felt that the nursing father of our infant Church had been taken from us."

A leading article in the "Polynesian" journal of Honolulu, in announcing the King's death, says,—

"His late Majesty was born on the 9th of February, 1834, and was therefore 29 years, 9 months, and 21 days old when he died. His mother was Kinau, the daughter of Kamehameha the Great, and his father is our venerable Governor Kekuanoa. An anecdote is related that when Liholiho was born, Kauikeaouli was so prepossessed with the babe, that he wrote on the door-sill that he should be called his

---

[2] The *Kahili* resembles a broom. The handle, composed of native wood, is ten or twelve feet long. Birds' feathers, yellow or dark, are fastened round the end which is held uppermost.

child and heir. He was afterwards formally adopted as his successor to the throne; and on the death of Kauikeaouli, December 15th, 1854, in accordance with that choice, he was proclaimed King. His reign thus extended a few days less than nine years. In June, 1856, he was married to Emma Rooke, who survives him. They had but one child, the late Prince of Hawaii, whose death, a little more than a year ago, robbed the nation of the fond hopes that it had placed in him as their future Sovereign.

"It is not the fit time nor place here, while the nation is still unrecovered from the first shock of grief at the announcement of the death of their King, to make a review of his short reign, or to pass an eulogium on him: that should be reserved for the future. But we cannot omit to speak here of one act of his short and eventful reign, which will place his name and that of his noble Queen Emma in letters of gold on the pages of his country's history—and this is the design and successful completion of the benevolent institution known as the Queen's Hospital. To the united efforts of the late King and his Queen it owes its origin, and now stands there, a monument of their sympathy and love for their wasting people. Well do we remember seeing him, in 1859, going alone and unattended through our streets, from house to house, and from store to store, with his memorandum book, and how the addition of $50 or $100 to his subscription list brightened up his countenance, and cheered him on in his good work till he saw some $6,000 pledged to second him in his noble undertaking. You, reader, may remember his quiet, earnest bearing, as he asked you to ' allow him the honour of setting your name down for any amount you might choose to give,' accompanying his request by a genial smile or by some lively remark. As long as that coral building stands and serves as a hospital, so long will the names of Kamehameha IV. and Queen Emma be cherished and venerated by all their people.

" On Tuesday the body of the late King lay in state at the palace, and was visited by thousands of foreigners and natives. The palace gates were heavily draped in black, after the style adopted at the death of Kauikeaouli and the young Prince. Both sides of the broad avenue were lined with household troops, and the steps leading to the verandahs with the Honolulu Rifles (of which company his Majesty was Colonel). At the door of the hall, staff officers received the visitors, and passed them to the reception or throne room, in which the body lay in state. Arranged

ROYAL MAUSOLEUM, HONOLULU

about it were four large candelabras, burning numerous wax candles, and vases of flowers. In attendance on the body were the family of the deceased, chiefs acting as kahili bearers; ministers and high state officers; members of lodges *Le Progrès de l'Océanie* and *Hawaiian* No. 21, F. and A. M., and other friends of the Royal Family. Then passing again into the hall, and out of the opposite door, the same disposition was made as to troops, through the rear gate into palace walk. In the yard we noticed an old native repeating, in a low monotonous manner, an ancient *mele*[3]. Crowds of natives were in attendance from first to last. Loud wailing was heard on every quarter, and wherever the eye turned every thing conveyed the sad intelligence that another of the Kamehamehas had passed to his long home."

The funeral did not take place for above two months, during which time a new mausoleum was erected, where might repose not only the remains of Kamehameha the Fourth, but of his predecessors and other high chiefs. It was solemnly consecrated a few

---

[3] When a chief dies, his dependants and other friends in succession recite their *meles*, or songs, often composed by themselves in praise of the deceased, recounting the deeds of his ancestors, and invoking the spots in the islands connected with his history.

days before the funeral, on the King's petition, which was read by the Minister of the Interior. "The funeral procession," says a letter, written by one of the clergy to friends in England, "moved from the palace about 10 a.m. on Wednesday, February 3rd. It was on foot, except that three carriages followed the royal coffin, to convey the Queen and other ladies of the Royal Family. Even the new King walked, followed by his ministers and principal officers of state. Immediately before the hearse went the ministers of religion of the several denominations, the Roman Catholic clergy, the Bishop of Arathea and Vicar Apostolic, the officiating clergy, and the Bishop of Honolulu. On arriving at the temporary cathedral the body was met by the Bishop and clergy, and the opening sentences were sung as the procession entered and moved towards the altar. The bier was raised six feet from the floor, and approached on all sides by steps. Over this had been erected a canopy, draped in black, round the cornice of which were written the words, 'I know that my Redeemer liveth.' The crown, sword, and hat of the late King were placed on the velvet pall, which had been embroidered with the Hawaiian coat of arms—a voluntary offering.

"At the head of the coffin knelt the widowed Queen Emma, and at the side his Majesty the King, the rest of the mourners, and the Court. The Psalm, 'I said, I will take heed,' &c., was chanted by the Bishop, clergy, and choir. The Lesson was beautifully read by an Hawaiian lawyer, whom the Bishop has licensed as a lay-preacher. The late King being regarded as the father of the infant Church, and himself a regular communicant, it was thought fitting to celebrate the Holy Communion, which was done chorally, the Queen receiving. With the exception of the *Gloria in excelsis*, Creed, and *Agnus Dei*, the whole service was in Hawaiian. Even the two chorales, 'I shall not in the grave remain,' and 'To Thee, O Lord, I yield my spirit,' from the *St. Paul* of Mendelssohn, and which were very effectively sung by a choir of fifty-two voices, had been translated into the native language. The church was hung with black, and on the walls were shields, bearing the following inscriptions :— 'Jesu, mercy,' 'Resurgam,' 'De profundis,' &c., and other similar phrases in Hawaiian. The Rev. J. J. Elkington, recently ordained a deacon, presided at the organ. When the body left the church, the Dead March was played. The procession then removed to the new mausoleum, one mile distant, where the rest of the service was performed. The " Polynesian " says,—

"'On Wednesday, February 3, according to proclamation, the last sad and solemn tribute of respect was paid to the remains of his late Majesty Kamehameha, 'Fourth' of the name, grandson of Kamehameha the Great, the founder of political unity and of civilization in the Hawaiian group, the seventh in succession from Keawe, the seventy-seventh in succession from Wakea, the one hundred and sixth in succession from Kane and Kaneloa, according to the genealogy of the ancient Hawaiian bards.

"'All that his exalted station did require, all that human love could devise to render this solemn event imposing in its outward arrangements and productive of the profoundest emotions, was done by willing hearts and unsparing hands. No funeral *cortége* of sovereign prince or noble chief in this country ever surpassed that of the late sovereign in the magnificence of its materials, the appropriateness of its designs, and the touching expression of deep sorrow and fond regret which it awakened in all beholders.

"'The tomb, lately erected of coral stone, in Gothic style, forms the western wing of what is intended, when finished, to be a mausoleum of the Royal Family; and its situation is one of the loveliest spots that could possibly have been chosen [4].

"'After a sharp rain during the previous night, the day of the funeral proved one of those magnificent ones in which our tropical climate is so rich. At sunrise, the battery on Punch-bowl-hill commenced firing minute guns, and so continued until the ceremony at the tomb was concluded. Every flag and ensign throughout the city and in the harbour trailed low at half-mast, stores and business places were shut, and up to the hour when the procession began to be formed, the streets wore an aspect of reverential silence—a most touching and appropriate prelude to the solemn event of the after hours. When the hour for forming the procession had struck, however, and the various bodies composing it began to collect in the places allotted them, the streets began to throng with eager and anxious spectators; walls, windows, balconies, verandahs, the very roofs of houses in the streets through which the procession moved, were lined with people; and, emerging out of town into the more open country, all spots within

---

[4] This building has since been completed at the expense of the Legislature.

reach along the road—rocks, walls, trees even—were crowded with occupants.

"'Out of a public procession so large, reaching nearly from Kawaiahao Church to within a short distance of the corner of Nuuanu and King Streets, in which every public and private association and every class of the community were represented, it would be invidious to remark upon the keeping and appearance of any one; but we believe that all will agree with us, that the most touching aspect of the procession was that of the 800 children who, with their teachers, had walked into Honolulu on that day, many from a long distance, to testify their love and regret, and their gratitude to the memory of a prince to whose heart their cause was ever the nearest.'"

The following remarks of Archdeacon Mason, in the sermon which he preached the Sunday after the King's death, will be read with interest:—

"As a Christian minister, could I have ventured to speak of the rest of the departed, had I not felt assured that he had found his rest in that only refuge of sinners, his crucified Redeemer? You may not all know how he loved communion with his Lord. You may not all know how it was his delight in the early morn to enter the courts of the Lord's house and partake of the bread of life, after due preparation and hearty contrition for past sin. Truly to him it was the most comfortable Sacrament of the Body and Blood of Christ. He ever looked upon the Holy Communion Service as a sacrifice of thanksgiving, which it was his 'bounden duty' to offer on all special occasions, whether of sorrow or of joy. Thus, when, but a few weeks ago, God visited him and his beloved Queen with a severe accident, his first thought was to send for his Bishop to celebrate privately those holy mysteries as a mark of his gratitude, and to express his consciousness of hourly dependence on the protecting hand of the King of kings.

"Nor need we fear that all this was formal superstition. The man who could appreciate Charles Kingsley's writings, and find keen pleasure in the poetry of Tennyson and Longfellow, is not likely to be the slave of forms and ceremonies. No! he would have worship indeed surrounded by all those accessories which can help to make it the more meet for the acceptance of the King to whom it is offered. But worship was to him the crown of life. He felt there must be a life in some measure prepared to receive that crown. And such was his. His life, at least for the past year, was a labour of love. Scarce can I trust myself to speak of that labour of sorrow, too, which the royal parents have had to bear these past weary months. Yet, when considering his labours, we must surely recall this, the heaviest of all—the loss of his fondest hope. . . . . Notwithstanding, you know how manfully he tried to shake off his natural grief, that he might do his duty as a Christian King and friend of the people, despite of physical infirmities and continually recurring depression of spirits. The advent of our mission, at a time when the first burst of grief had scarce subsided, could but really have added weight to the burden he had to bear. But his refined, unselfish spirit never allowed his manner to betray the feeling that now one great source of joy at the arrival of our Mission was dried up for ever. No! his words, his manner, his deeds ever spoke welcome! welcome! To use his own kind poetry of expression, 'our coming was,' he said, 'as the evening dew on the sun-scorched flowers.' Nor must we omit to notice here the fear his sensitive soul must have felt on being obliged to manifest his deliberate adoption of a system of worship and education which he was convinced was the best adapted to his people, lest by so doing he should appear to show ingratitude to those many benevolent persons who had sought to benefit his native race, though by means of religious systems he himself could not sympathize with. How much he suffered in this way few can tell; but many ought to be able to appreciate the delicacy which made him so anxious not to offend the feelings of any who might differ from him politically or religiously, by the introduction of any measures calculated to have such an effect. His thoughtful mind saw what was the work God had given him to do, and he did it—wisely, gently, devotedly. And connected with this work of planting our Mission, how many collateral works occupied his time and thoughts, and called forth his living and active sympathy! . . . The translation of our Book of Common Prayer into the native language was by no means an amusement for his leisure hours. He gave himself to the work as to a real, important work for God; and, as if prescient of the coming end, he could not rest satisfied until it was accomplished. That book, with its thoughtful preface, shall remain a monument of his piety, his wisdom, and his love for his people. The glorious consequences of this thy noble work, Iolani, shall follow thee to doom!

"How many bright remembrances besides those we have already recalled, rise up worthy of record as a supplement to the acts of the Royal Saints of Christendom,—remembrances culled not only from the past brief year of good works, when the principle of good within him may be said to have developed, and to have been moulded more definitely, more fixedly—but also from bygone years, when that same principle was evidently energizing, but oftentimes, no doubt, checked or turned aside by the impetuous rush of passions which inadequate education and training could not enable him sufficiently to control [5]. Thus, how pleasing it is now to hear of the tender anxiety he felt for his race when that terrible small-pox visited these islands! Regardless of infection, he entered their huts, and did all he could to relieve their necessities. When he ascended the throne, he would not be content till a hospital was raised as a refuge for his disease-afflicted people. And to achieve this, many of you remember how he begged from door to door with royal humility for those dollars his own limited exchequer was unable to furnish! May it not be said of him as of Cornelius the Centurion, 'his prayers and alms had

---

[5] The last thought of my reverend brother was to attribute any blame to the early instructors of his late Majesty.—T. N. H.

gone up as a memorial before God'? Hence was he prepared to add to his good works a modest faith in the Church and her ordinances. Hence the secret of his Christmas joy last year, when the blazing kukui torches revealed in the streets of his royal city the unwonted sight of a King walking in choral procession at midnight, hymning the nativity of the Babe of Bethlehem. Hence he felt it rather an honour than a condescension to robe himself in the white robe of the sanctuary, when no priest was with him last spring on the island of Hawaii, that he might pray with his people out of our translated office-book, and speak to them words of warning and of hope. Brethren, I must pause. Your own memories may help many of you to fill up from the details of daily life the description of a man who will ever be endeared to us as a gentleman monarch and a Christian brother. Let us not, brethren, be surprised if we hear some refer to the failings of the deceased King in contradiction to the words of eulogium that have been spoken of his character. The imperfections even of some of God's great saints have been found sufficient, for a time at least, to blight their pious memories. There always will be found some who disregard the wholesome proverb of charity, 'De mortuis nil nisi bonum.' Should you meet with any such, brethren, recommend to their meditations the Saviour's parable of the two men who went up into the temple to pray—the one a Pharisee, and the other a Publican. Suggest to them the study of that King of Israel, the "man after God's own heart," the "sweet psalmist of Israel," THE ROYAL PENITENT—who, out of the fulness of his contrite heart, gave expression to this truth of God, to be the confidence of all penitents while the world shall last: 'The sacrifices of God are a broken spirit; a broken and contrite heart, O God, thou wilt not despise.'"

. .

Many were the letters of sympathy addressed from England to the widowed Queen by persons eminent both in the Church and in the State. Our own beloved Sovereign, with her characteristic tenderness, was among the first to write to Queen Emma words of condolence and comfort. Keble, who had always taken a deep interest in the Mission, was deeply moved at the news of the King's death; and in a letter, enclosing another, intended to console the royal widow, wrote thus to the Bishop:—

"I know you will give us credit for not having left

you and Mrs. Staley unthought of, either in your work, or in your deep afflictions at home [6] and in the Church, the one, doubtless, the more blessed from the other. A high privilege surely has been yours . . . . has been and is . . . . to wait upon, and guide and encourage those truly royal ones, who seem to have realized, and to be still realizing, more completely than I remember ever to have read in history, the prophetic image of a nursing Father and a nursing Mother— not affecting to patronize the Church, but counting it their joy and glory to be head-servants to her in her nursery, tending her children, and trying to protect, and shelter, and bring them up for her. My wife has persuaded me that it might be worth while to write a few lines of respectful condolence to your good and noble Queen Emma. I have tried to do so, and forward the attempt in this cover; but, my dear Lord, I must depend entirely upon your great kindness to deliver or suppress it as you may judge most seasonable. To offer consolation under such circumstances of distress, is a kind of venture, even with our nearest acquaintance, and may well seem a mere impertinence when one is at such a distance in

---

[6] This refers to a bereavement in the Bishop's family the previous year.

every sense. I can only say, however, it is quite sincere."

Keble little thought that within a year and a half from the date of this letter, "the distance" of which he spoke would have vanished, and Queen Emma be listening in the Parsonage at Hursley to him whose "Christian Year" she had found so great a comfort in her deepest sorrows.

V.

POSITION OF THE CHURCH SINCE THE DEATH OF KAMEHAMEHA IV.—ITS WORK.

THE new King, who had acted as Minister of the Interior through the whole of his brother's reign, lost no time in assuring the Bishop of his friendly intentions. "I regard the Church as a sacred legacy bequeathed by my predecessor"—such were his words on the day of his accession. His Majesty, too, expressed his earnest wish "to use the Bishop's experience" in raising the character of the State schools. With this view, the Bishop was subsequently placed on the Privy Council of State, and nominated a member of the Board of Education. His Majesty also promised his pecuniary aid to the Mission—a promise which he afterwards amply fulfilled.

Convinced that the Constitution granted in 1852 by his uncle[1] was far too democratic for a people so

---

[1] Under the influence of the Congregationalist Mission.

recently emancipated from feudalism and arbitrary government, he proceeded to convoke a Council of Delegates to consult with him on the subject. Elections were held all over the kingdom of representatives to serve in this "Convention." The cry which an unscrupulous opposition, headed by a few of the more violent and political of the American missionaries, got up, was, that the King wished to alter the Constitution, to enable him "to tax his subjects $5 each for the support of the English Church!" This was commonly believed, and did more than any thing else to thwart the object of the Convention. The pulpits of Congregational preachers, native and American, rang with tirades against the Bishop and clergy. It was every where stated that the Prince and King had died, because of *their* presence in the islands. "The fates, in fact, were against the Church; and such plagues would continue to befall the land till the nuisance had been got rid of." The King made a progress through the Islands, accompanied by his faithful minister, Mr. Wyllie, and everywhere contradicted these false and wicked fabrications. It is interesting to find the King, during this progress, having service on board his yacht each Sunday, saying the prayers *himself* from the Hawaiian Prayer Book which his own brother had translated, and encouraging his subjects to join the Anglican Church. The majority, however, elected as the Convention was, by the credulous natives, under such misrepresentations, proved refractory.

After a session of seven weeks, His Majesty dissolved the Convention, and proclaimed a new Constitution, based on an intelligence and property qualification for voters [2]. This Constitution proved most acceptable to the community, excepting to the same noisy faction. The many falsehoods disseminated in the Islands were believed and adopted by the American Congregational Missionary Society at Boston, U.S., and a " Report," published there, was circulated in the Islands, directed against " The Episcopal Mission." This led the Bishop to deliver a Pastoral Address, on New Year's Day, 1865, in the presence of their Majesties the King and Queen, and a large congregation, vindicating himself and the Mission generally from the charges of *intrusion*, of having a *political* character, and from other absurd allegations.

The visit of the good Queen Emma to England the same year is too fresh in the memories of Churchmen in England and the United States to require any but

[2] See in Appendix a copy of it.

a passing notice here[3]. What is now proposed, is to describe the work which is being done at the four stations of the Church, beginning with—

Honolulu.

Here, at the capital, situated in the island of Oahu, is a population of from thirteen to fourteen thousand, of whom nearly one-fourth are foreigners, chiefly British, American, and German residents. Services are therefore held, on Sundays and daily throughout the week, in both the Hawaiian and English languages. The composite character of the population adds, of course, greatly to the labours of the limited clerical staff employed in this city. Besides the Bishop, who is occasionally absent on his episcopal and missionary visitations, there are only two clergymen stationed there, one of whom is fully occupied as Master of St. Alban's College[4], where Hawaiian and other boys of a higher class are being educated in the English language. The boarders, who form the majority of the scholars, are assembled in a little chapel attached to the institution, morning and even-

[3] See Appendix.
[4] Built by the late King for the girls' boarding school, which is now carried on near the church.

S. ALBAN'S COLLEGE FOR BOYS, NUUANU VALLEY, HONOLULU.

himself; but it does not include a variety of other calls upon the members of the congregation in the form of subscriptions for special objects—take, for example, the one at Christmas, 1866, which amounted to 30*l*., and was devoted to the Female Industrial School at Lahaina. Nor does it include upwards of another 200*l*. a year devoted by His Majesty out of his own purse to the education of boys and girls in the several English schools of the Mission. It has been even a source of complaint among those who manage the Hawaiian "Civil List," that the Church is a continued drain on the King's very limited resources. With an income which would be thought very modest for a country squire in England, we have Kamehameha V. devoting upwards of 400*l*. a year to the cause of education and religion. By this readiness to sacrifice so largely of his own substance in the cause of the Church, he gives the most convincing proof of the value which he attaches to its presence in his kingdom.

The attention of the Hawaiian Government had long been directed to the value of Industrial Boarding Schools for girls; and the Board of Education, of which the Bishop was appointed a member by the present King, arranged in 1865 a system of capitation grants, with a view to encourage their formation and aid in their maintenance. The rules under which the Board assists schools of this kind were drawn up by the Bishop, and have met with general acceptance and approval. One of them is, "Convinced that religion is the basis of all sound moral training, the Board expects that such schools shall be conducted on Christian principles; but it leaves to their directors full discretion as to the form of Christianity they may feel it right to inculcate." The result has been greatly to multiply these establishments in the Islands, so that the last year's Educational Report stated there were already *fivefold* as many children under training in female boarding schools as there were previously. It is evident that the evils which not only militated so fearfully against the prosperity of the nation, but threatened its speedy extinction, are being fairly grappled with. In bringing about this happier state of things, it is pleasing to find the English Mission has taken a leading part. The sisters and wives of the clergy from the first devoted themselves, as far as they could, to the training of Hawaiian girls, both at Lahaina and Honolulu. And now at both places are "Sisters of Mercy," who have gone out from this country for the purpose of spending their lives in this noble work [5]. The first institution of the kind placed under their management was that at Lahaina, in 1865. It is now filled to overflowing, and applications for admission have to be refused. It receives between 200*l*. and 300*l*. yearly in the shape of capitation grants.

To Miss Sellon, the foundress of sisterhoods in our Reformed Church, the Bishop is indebted for this most valuable branch of Missionary work. Finding the one at Lahaina so complete a success, this lady, though in a weak state of health, at a great sacrifice of time and money, visited Honolulu last year, for the purpose of undertaking the conduct of a similar institution there. She expended on suitable buildings, and in the purchase of land, upwards of 1400*l*. out of her own resources for this benevolent object; and she received the thanks of the King in person for the benefits which her "sisterhood" had conferred upon his people.

After her return to England, last July, Miss Sellon addressed to the Bishop a letter, recording her agreeable impressions of the people, the King, the Queen, and the general work of the Mission:—

"Shall I," says the writer, "ever forget that love-

[5] See Appendix.

S. ANDREW'S PRIORY, HONOLULU, FOR THE SISTERHOOD AND GIRLS' BOARDING SCHOOL.

liest and most interesting of islands on the day of the Confirmation held in the lowly but beautifully-arranged little church, built beside the sounding waves of the Pacific? Dear little church! How lovingly was it adorned by native hands with wreaths of the elegant Datura, and with what devout and earnest attention did the congregation witness the solemn rite, and how happy our children were!

"You ask me my impressions of the people. Their affectionate manners, their agreeable vivacity, and ever-ready cordiality were, I think, charming, especially when added to their poetical love of the beautiful. It is to be hoped that the fictitious wants and increase of cares, &c., which higher degrees of civilization will bring, will not destroy these characteristics. Whether it is possible to hope for a higher standard of morals, without further education, is doubtful. Evidently the King, whose devotion to the welfare of his country, and whose intellectual power and wisdom in government are unquestionable, believes in the efficacy of education for meeting the present requirements of the people. The Queen's opinion is, if I mistake not, the same, and you also, I am aware, feel deeply and keenly on the subject. I know your anxiety for the increase of the schools for both boys and girls, and your wish to enlarge them. As far as I am concerned, I hope to do all in my power to forward this object.

"Careful education may by God's blessing diminish anxiety respecting the health and longevity of the people. It is encouraging to observe the excellent health of the children of our Mission boarding-schools; and encouraging also is the fact, because it betokens some strength of constitution; that our climate, so different from the sunny skies of their lovely Islands, does not at all injuriously affect my adopted little Hawaiian daughters, who are educating here, to return again, if it please God to spare them to me, as home missionaries to their country [6]. There is a reasonable hope that by careful cultivation and by attention to the sanitary measures the King is adopting, the longevity of the people may in the course of generations be equal to our own. It is said that the natives must perish; but I do not see why this is to be assumed as a reason for apathy in this particular instance, or why energy in attempting to avert so great a catastrophe as the extinction of this fine people is to be damped, as though we had been

---

[6] Miss Sellon has four little Hawaiian girls in England under her care, whom she brought with her from the Islands.

HOSPITAL OF S. CROSS, FOR THE SISTERHOOD AND INDUSTRIAL GIRLS' SCHOOL, LAHAINA.

told on irrefragable evidence that the hour is at hand.

"More reasonably might we say that, man being born to die, we should treat with indifference the warnings of some illness, which nothing but our own carelessness need render mortal.

"People assume as a fact that the Hawaiian race must die out. They may as well, first of all, try (as the King is doing) whether it is the will of Heaven that it should survive.

"A few words as to our Mission. Chiefly I was impressed with the quiet, simple beauty of the services, and the care that was taken that the musical part of them should be such as all could join in and appreciate—so important there. All who attended the services seemed to enjoy and value them. Some of the happiest hours I ever had were those early celebrations for the native congregation. How one felt the realization of the promise that the ends of the earth shall see the salvation of our God; and, as in the hearty and reverent service the musical accents of the Hawaiian tongue fell on one's ear, that in the Church all nations and people are one kindred! You know, too, how much I valued—for I think I often expressed it to you—the union of the full teaching of the Catholic Faith with the calm simplicity of the ritual you there adopted, calculated as far as possible to soothe the troubled surging of men's minds, which now agitates even the remotest shores where the Church of Christ is planted, creating difficulties which can only be judged of or estimated on the spot, and even there, probably, only by those whose position calls upon them to love, and bear with, and minister to all alike, and with equal consideration. Of this, and of manifold and remarkable trials and drawbacks, which beset the first years of the Mission, it is not for me to venture to write; but I may observe that the finest of our forest trees is of the slowest growth, and that it is not in six, nor sixteen, nor, perhaps, sixty years, that the fruit of the late pious King's prayers, and thoughts, and exertions to plant the Mission will appear—probably not until long after all its founders and first members have ceased from earthly labour. How happy to be permitted to sow the seed, if hereafter others who enter into the field find that God has given the increase!

"The perfectly restored health of the Queen was to me great encouragement. She, so beloved by the people, and so loving them, is a centre on which one's thoughts fix, under God, with reference to the work of the Church in the Islands. God has apparently given her so entire a submission to His Will, that the cup of anguish which He, in mysterious love, gave her to drink, has never embittered to her life or its affections. Living amidst her people, ever ready to give cheerful attention with that peculiar fresh sweetness so exclusively her own, one cannot but feel that to her the time of her deepest sorrow has arrived, because, to all human eyes, her deepest sorrow is past. This very powerfully struck me, in one whose young life of an almost singular happiness has been so suddenly and so irremediably stricken. She is the joy of her people's heart, in a way which must be witnessed to be in the least understood.

"Remembrances of deep interest crowd upon me; but I have already written at greater extent than I had intended. The affectionateness of the Hawaiians to ourselves was very pleasant at all times; the genial smile and welcome was ever ready. I remember on Holy Thursday, after the morning service, just as the gate of the Priory (the new building) was being put up, how the native congregation poured in, offering the ring of friendship, and the many congratulatory clasps of the hand on the completion of the work, with their beaming smiles, and ever sweet 'alohas.'

And then on that last day the kindly aloha and their parting gifts, betokening their love and value for the dear ones I left behind, who, I felt, were surrounded with loving hearts. Dear, kind-hearted, loving people! May the best of blessings be theirs!

"Believe me, my dear Lord,
"Yours very faithfully,
"Priscilla Lydia Sellon."

Lahaina.

The Female Industrial Boarding School, referred to already, is by no means the only feature of interest. Archdeacon Mason, assisted by an American clergyman, carries on there an English school for boys, supported mainly by the Board of Education. This is in addition to the spiritual work of the Mission, which with services, as at Honolulu, in both the English and the Hawaiian language, is far from light. He has above eighty boys, of whom twenty-five are boarders. The object which Mr. Mason has in view is to give a thorough education, in English, to Hawaiian boys. It is a sad commentary on the forty years' nominal Christianity of these Islands, as well as on the native schools, that the business of the Government, from the ministers down to the petty magistrate, or even the sheriff's officer, has to be entrusted, with few exceptions, to Europeans or Americans. Little progress can be expected among a people with a language so inadequate in its vocabulary and its literature as is the Hawaiian; nor through it as a medium can those right ideas and principles be implanted which are essential to any one who desires to fulfil offices of trust either in the Church or in the State. The Government apprentice a number of picked and promising youths to this school, as well as to the one at Honolulu, in the hope of seeing hereafter a body of intelligent and trustworthy men educated in the English language, taught to think and reason in English, and familiar with English literature, and able to take a part in administering the government and judiciary of the kingdom. Equally beneficial may these schools be expected to prove to the Church itself. Here and there will be found among the scholars youths who may be expected to fill the ranks of the future native ministry. For, unless the Church is to be a mere exotic, she must look forward to that as the great object of her mission. A ministry that has been schooled in English thought and English *morality*, and received its dogmas through a tongue adequate to express them, will be much safer guides in things

F

spiritual than they would otherwise be, although they may have to employ only the vernacular when they are called upon to impart religious instruction to their fellow-countrymen.

Both Mr. and Mrs. Mason have rendered signal service to the Mission at Lahaina by the self-denial, devotion, and zeal with which, under many difficulties, they have laboured for the social, physical, and moral elevation of the people. A permanent stone church is much wanted here, instead of the miserable shed now used for Divine Service.

Kona (Hawaii).

The Rev. C. G. Williamson, trained at S. Augustine's, Canterbury, and ordained Deacon by the Bishop of Oxford, assisted by the Bishop of North Carolina, who was then in England, arrived in the Islands in March, 1867, to take part in the Mission. In a private letter, of which public use is allowed to be made, he thus recorded his impressions of the first Sunday which he spent in Honolulu :—

"Oh, how I wish that some of our English friends could have been present at the service of that morning ! The example set by the natives, as regards devo-

KEALAKEKUA BAY (KONA)

tion and joining in the service, would shame many a congregation in England. You could hear the responses echoed from all parts of the church while the Canticles and Psalms were chanted in Hawaiian, in good taste and with much feeling. And so it was at the English service, attended by many formerly Presbyterians, Methodists, and American Episcopalians. Each member of the congregation seemed to pour out his whole soul in worship. Our hymns were heart-stirring and full of devotion; and my thoughts were carried back to dear old England when I recognized familiar chants and tunes."

After studying the language for a few months, and assisting at Honolulu, Mr. Williamson went to the Island of Hawaii; and near Kealakekua Bay, where Captain Cook fell in 1779, opened a Mission. An English resident gave two acres of land for the erection of the required buildings, which have now been completed. They consist of a neat Gothic church and school, and clergy-house. Both among the foreign residents, chiefly Englishmen, who are farmers, graziers, or mechanics, as well as among the native people, his labours are being crowned with a reasonable measure of success. The district of Kona, in the west of the island, where his station is situated, was much shaken and damaged by the late severe earthquakes, though, happily, the buildings were not destroyed, nor any lives lost in his district, the effects being felt most in the south-eastern extremity of the island [7].

WALUKU MAUI.

The value of American co-operation in the Mission to North Polynesia had been felt by its friends and promoters from the first. There are many settlers in the Hawaiian Islands from the United States engaged in developing their industry and trade. The first evangelizers of the people were New England Puritans; and in the absence of the "Episcopal Church," some who at home had been baptized and trained in the American branch of it were induced to frequent their ministrations, while others sought a refuge in the Roman communion. Accordingly, before the establishment of the Bishopric was completed, the Bishops of California and New York, who happened to be in London, were consulted, and they expressed their conviction that "England's daughter-Church in their own country would gladly take a part in the work of the Mission." This was stated in the first

[7] See Appendix.

prospectus which was issued on the subject. The great fratricidal war, however, which just then broke out in the United States, and absorbed the whole attention of that nation, rendered any immediate realization of this scheme impossible.

The Bishop, on his arrival at Honolulu in 1862, found political feeling running very high between the American and English residents, intensified, as is usually the case, by the distance of these communities from their parent centres. Of the English in Hawaii many were partisans of the South; but the majority of the Americans were from New England. The Bishop carefully abstained from any expressions of sympathy with either side in that great conflict, while he sought to allay these national asperities by praying at the English services for "the President of the United States," equally with "her Britannic Majesty." His moderation bore its natural fruit. One of the first whom he confirmed was the King's Attorney-General, now Minister of Finance, a native of New Hampshire. Others of the American residents became regular attendants and communicants, and have been steady in their attachment to the Church at Honolulu ever since. When the news arrived of the assassination of President Lincoln, the church was immediately draped in black, a special memorial service was held, and a funeral sermon preached by an American clergyman, who had come over as a visitor—the building being filled with a body of reverent worshippers, who were no less touched by the thoughtful sympathy of an English Bishop than by the appropriate solemnity of the observances. Still the American Congregationalists continued to reiterate the oft-refuted assertion that " Bishop Staley was only an emissary of the London Foreign Office, sent out to secure the annexation of the Islands to the British Empire"—a statement which, absurd as it may seem, was too commonly believed. Had, however, any thing further been required to disabuse these opponents of such a prejudice, they might have found it in the proceedings of the Bishop in 1865, when, immediately on the close of the Civil War, he paid a visit to the United States to attend the General Convention of the Church at Philadelphia. It was the one which excited so much interest here from the circumstance that the Southern Bishops, for the first time since the General Convention at Richmond, in 1859, met with their Northern brethren, and were received, on entering the Council chamber, with a burst of joy and welcome, which only found its expression in the singing of the "Gloria in Excelsis." On the fourteenth day of the session, in the Upper House, Bishop Staley spoke on the subject of his Mission, and presented a letter addressed to the American prelates, from the King, respectfully inviting their sympathy and co-operation.

The following is a minute taken from the Report of the General Convention of 1865 relating to this subject:—

"Bishop STEVENS, at the close of the Bishop of Honolulu's address, said,—

"'The House of Bishops, having listened with interest to the statements of the Right Rev. the Bishop of Honolulu, in reference to the moral and religious condition of the Hawaiian Islands, and to the present state and future needs of his Mission, take pleasure in assuring the Bishop of their desire to do what may properly be in their power to aid him in his work of making known to the foreign and native residents of that kingdom the doctrine, discipline, and worship of the Church as jointly held by the Church of England and the Protestant Episcopal Church of the United States of America.'

"*Resolved*, That the House of Bishops receives

with sincere pleasure the letter of Kamehameha V. to this House, and begs leave to assure His Majesty that they earnestly desire to extend to his kingdom the full blessings of the Gospel of Christ, and their sincere hope that he may, by the grace of God, prove to be a nursing father to the Church of the living God in the Hawaiian Islands.

"*Resolved,* That the Presiding Bishop be requested to convey to His Majesty this expression of the regard of the House of Bishops, and that the letter of the King be entered on the Journal, and the original be deposited with the Registrar of the General Convention."

The following is the letter which Kamehameha addressed to the House of Bishops:—

"Molokai, August, 1866.

"*To the Bishops of the Church of the United States now assembled in General Convention.*

"RIGHT REVEREND FATHERS IN GOD,—Understanding that my friend and chaplain the Bishop of Honolulu is about to visit the United States of America, in order to create an interest there in his work, and obtain men and means for carrying it on more extensively, I have taken the liberty of making known to you how greatly I sympathize in the objects he has in view.

"From his Mission to these Islands great practical good to my people has arisen. The Liturgy, Constitution, and teaching of the Episcopal Church seems to me more consistent with monarchy than any other form of Christianity that I have met with; and the principles of education it inculcates seem to me, from practical evidence before my eye, to have the effect of making its members more moral, religious, and loyal citizens.

"The system of the family training it adopts in female schools is admirably fitted to cure a great social evil of this land.

"There can by the Constitution be no Church supported by the State in Hawaii; but nothing could give me greater pleasure than to find the Church, invited hither by my late lamented brother, widely spreading and taking root in my kingdom.

"I am, Right Reverend Fathers,

"Yours faithfully,

"KAMEHAMEHA."

That this letter elicited a favourable response on the part of the American House of Bishops is not a matter of surprise, nor that the Bishop of Honolulu felt it necessary to exhibit private letters which he had received from the King, to prove that one whose grandfather was an illiterate barbarian could pen such a document. The Board of Missions at once pledged half-stipends for *two* American clergymen to work under the Bishop's jurisdiction; though, in consequence of difficulties arising from the constitution of the Board, it was thought better that the resolution should be carried into effect by the formation of an independent Committee, on which the late Presiding Bishop, and the Bishops of New York, Connecticut, Minnesota, New Jersey, Maine, and Pittsburg, placed their names. There are now two American missionaries working under the Bishop in the Islands. The Rev. G. B. Whipple, brother of the Bishop of Minnesota, opened his station early in 1866, at Wailuku Maui, and collected on the spot at once a sum of $900 for the purpose, the King making over an excellent site of two acres on which to erect suitable Mission-buildings. No one in so short a time could have succeeded better than Mr. Whipple. He had lived in his youth some years in one of the Islands before he was ordained, and had learnt the language, and been trained under his brother in missionary life among the Indians. In May last the Bishop held his second visitation there—an event described so well by Mrs. Whipple in a periodical of the United States, that we print her letter in full, showing as it does the extent of the work which has been accomplished, and the part the good Queen Emma takes in aiding the Mission:—

"Our island life has been varied during this month by two events of interest: the visit of Queen Emma and her suite to Wailuku, and the visitation of the Bishop, the latter occurring during the last days of the Queen's stay.

"Her Majesty, accompanied by his Excellency Nahaolelua, Governor of this island, and Hon. Colonel Kalakana, and others from Honolulu, arrived on Tuesday, May 14th, and went to the Governor's house, where the natives soon began to flock with their offerings. It was quite touching to see them go by, with their gifts of eggs, bananas, fowls, fish, berries, sugar-cane, *taro*, and other vegetables, to lay at the feet of their 'Chief,' according to old custom— the outgrowth of the feudal feeling, which has not yet entirely died away.

"On Wednesday Her Majesty attended the early native service, and at ten o'clock received the boys of the Mission-school, who went in a body to pay their respects, and make their little offerings. The youngest of all—a pretty child of four years—as soon as one of the older boys had made his little speech introducing the others, evidently thinking it was time for him to be doing something, walked directly up to the Queen, and with a most confiding, yet timid air, gave the bunch of flowers which he had brought, and received a kind greeting from Her Majesty, whose simple dignity of manners is combined with the most winning graciousness towards her people.

"On Thursday Her Majesty and suite visited the different departments of the Mission day-schools. Her Majesty expressed herself particularly pleased that a boy of pure Hawaiian birth excelled in his class several half-caste boys.

"Friday evening, 17th, after the English service, the Queen visited the free evening-school for adult natives who wished to learn English. The Bishop also was present, although he had arrived from Lahaina after a tedious horseback-journey of twenty-five miles over the mountains, just as the last service-bell rang, and had come in immediately to service,

CLERGY HOUSE AND SCHOOL CHURCH, WAILUKU MAUI

and given an extemporaneous address, without any pause for rest or refreshment.

"There were some very interesting native meetings during the week, and at one or two of these the Hon. Colonel Kalakana, at the missionary's request, spoke to the congregation concerning the Church and her services. In speaking to them of postures to be observed, he remarked that he had seen many of them approach to ask a favour of their earthly king, when they would kneel, and even crawl in the humblest manner to his feet. 'And yet,' said he, 'can you think it proper to ask a favour of the King of kings, without any outward mark of respect, sitting upright when you are praying to Him?'

"On Saturday the missionary entertained at dinner, at the clergy-house, Her Majesty Queen Emma, the Governor of Maui, the Hon. Colonel Kalakana, and Judge Kahalewai, all members of the Church, and staunch supporters of it, meeting there with their Bishop, who was staying in the house.

"Sunday was a rainy day; but the chapel was well filled at each service. At nine o'clock the Hawaiian Litany was intoned by the Bishop, the congregation singing the responses, as usual, with great apparent zest and fervour. The Confirmation service followed this, and fourteen were presented for the rite. At English Morning Prayer the Bishop preached to a full and attentive audience, the Holy Communion being celebrated after the sermon.

"At the four p.m. Hawaiian service, the Bishop baptized three infants, Queen Emma standing sponsor for them. The English evening service was better attended than could have been expected, it being a wet, dark night. The Bishop gave a very interesting and pleasant talk about the Prayer Book.

"Tuesday morning, the 23rd, the Hawaiian communicants met for an early celebration of the Holy Eucharist. The Queen was present, and at the close of the service gave her parting *aloha* (ordinary salutation, expressing love and good-will) to her people. Soon after, Her Majesty and her party left Wailuku for Lahaina, on the other side of the mountain. The Bishop, too, left us, to take passage in a little schooner for Honolulu; and we returned to our ordinary round of schools and services, cheered and brightened not a little by the pleasant memories of the week just ended."

It is pleasant and encouraging to find one part of the great Mission field acting for good upon another.

Mr. and Mrs. Whipple, when living in Minnesota, adopted a little Indian girl, whom they have educated to that point that, except for her slight tinge of colour, she might now, at eighteen years of age, be mistaken for an English young lady. She acts as organist in church, and assistant-mistress in the English school.

There is much that addresses itself to the imagination, and touches the poetical sensibilities, in the annals of the English Mission to these Islands of the Pacific. But were that *all*, the result could hardly be deemed satisfactory. What must be the most gratifying thought to its friends and promoters, is, that a real solid work for good is being carried on, and specially in the education and training of those on whom, more than in the case of any previous generation, depends the question, whether the Hawaiian, at least as an unmixed, race, is or is not doomed to extinction.

But we may affirm that the beneficial influence of the Church is not to be measured by its direct effects alone. It is admitted by all intelligent residents in the Hawaiian kingdom, that the other religious denominations have been aroused by its example to greater efforts in the work of social and national reformation. The reverent and hearty worship of Hawaiian Churchmen is adduced by the Congregationalists in their native journals as worthy of imitation in their own places of meeting [8]. The great holidays of the Church are now *national* institutions, their existence before the arrival of the Bishop being all but unknown [9].

[8] See the "Kuokoa," Sept. 15, 1866 (a Native Congregational organ):—"It is a thing for us to be ashamed of, compared with the Episcopalians (Episekopo) and Roman Catholics, the sitting careless, and not bowing the head nor standing, when the minister prays." The passage then proceeds to compare the irreverence of Hawaiian worshippers in their meeting-houses now, with that of "the old Puritans."

[9] "For the last *five* years," says the Honolulu "Gazette" of January 1st of the present year, "our Christmas salutes have been fired from the fort on Punch-bowl Hill, and the official recognition of this great Christian anniversary has been made. It is now adopted as a *national* holiday, and becomes a national recognition of the claims of Christianity on the Government. It is a festival fraught with blessed memories."

The following notice was issued *last* Good Friday at Honolulu:—"Friday, April 10th, is the commemoration of the sufferings and Passion of our Lord Jesus Christ, and is *generally* observed by Christian nations. Therefore, notice is hereby given, no public business will be transacted on that day, and all Government offices will be closed throughout the kingdom." It is amusing to find the Congregationalist organ at Honolulu, which for a long time steadily set its face against these Catholic innovations, a few days later, April 11th, admitting, somewhat ungraciously, perhaps, the propriety of such observances. "The past week has been 'Holy Week' on the calendar of the *Ritualistic* (!) Churches. The bells of the cathedral were ringing vigorously on Thursday morning, and on Good Friday

And there has been a corresponding zeal on the part of the State in dealing with the moral evils of the country, which threatened, if unchecked by legislation, ere long to extinguish the Hawaiian race altogether. Under the wise and firm rule of the present King, the following measures have been brought into operation: "An Act to establish an Industrial and Reformatory School for neglected children, and for the reformation of juvenile offenders" (this school is conducted by a master sent out from England in 1863, to labour in connexion with the Mission); "An Act to regulate the Bureau of Public Instruction, and establish female schools;" "An Act to Facilitate the Proof of Marriage;" and "An Act to regulate the Carrying of Passengers between the Islands," the object of which may be inferred from the provision, that it "shall not be lawful for any vessel engaged in inter-island navigation to receive on board any female under twenty-five years of age, to convey her to Honolulu, without her having first delivered to the master of the vessel so employed a passport signed

the Government offices were closed .... an observance which, though strange to a large portion of the people, is, perhaps, less uncalled for, because many of our foreign residents at home used to notice the day. Easter Sunday, even in Protestant churches, is sometimes made occasion for appropriate exercises."

by some person duly authorized, which shall set forth the cause and probable duration of such visit"—a safeguard of immense value to the morals of the female population.

In 1862 there were only 51 girls in family *boarding-*schools; in 1867 there were 256. In 1862 there were 752 scholars in the *English* day-schools; in 1867 there were 1066. In the former year there was not a single school taught in the Hawaiian language where the girls were separated from the boys. All sat in the same room, and learnt and played together, a native young man often being their sole instructor —an arrangement most mischievous to their morals, and precluding any distinctive training for their sex. Now there are 24 schools of girls alone, each taught by a native mistress. These are well-authenticated, published statistics, and they may be, perhaps, regarded as testifying to the indirect benefits which the presence of an English Bishop (apart even from his more spiritual character), and of his coadjutors, has conferred on this little Island State.

VI.

DIFFICULTIES AND PROSPECTS.

IT has been already stated that a farewell service was held in Westminster Abbey on the eve of the departure of the Mission to the Islands. The Committee were of opinion that a few parting words from the Bishop might be then appropriately delivered on the nature and prospects of the work before him. The following is an extract from the sermon preached on the occasion :—

"Such, Brethren, are the chief outlines of the task we are undertaking. I cannot hide the fact that its accomplishment seems beset with difficulties and perils. If the ground were wholly unoccupied, as it was when we were first invited to take possession of it in Christ's name, the case would be very different from what it actually is. It is hoped that the introduction of that pure and complete development of

Divine truth it is our happiness as English Churchmen to enjoy, concentrating in its worship and teaching all that is good and beautiful and true, in the two extremes, without running into the excesses of either, may dispel some of those doubts, which systems so antagonistic as those now at work there, must have created in their minds. It may be so; but it may produce the contrary effect. And a vast responsibility devolves on those to whom is entrusted the direction of this sacred enterprise, to see that the former, and not the latter, be the result of their efforts. Nothing would shake all religious belief in the Islands more effectually than for us to assume an attitude of hostility to those forms of Christianity with which they are now familiar. We must show the people how, beneath the defects and corruptions of this or that communion, there lies a substratum of truth in the admission of the great historic facts of the Creeds, which may well increase their faith in those facts, and lead to greater charity and forbearance in our treatment of those Articles of the Faith which are called in question. We are to speak the truth, but it must be in love; and we are to give all who have been hitherto labouring with so much devotion and earnestness in their Master's cause, while we have been looking on with cold indifference, the credit they deserve. We must make it clear we do not go forth to ignore or over-ride what has been done by others.

"And this suggests another danger—that of seeking to proselytize. It is an admitted fact that a large number of the people are in active communion with none of the existing bodies, and among them we must seek to labour, not doubting that, as we thus exhibit and carry to them the Church's message in all fidelity and zeal and love, she will attract many others, whom she would effectually repel were she to assume a posture of unfriendliness or aggression. If we keep before our eyes the fact, that the great object of the Mission is the salvation of the souls and bodies of those among whom we are going to labour, and not the numbers we can count as members of our communion, we may hope, by God's blessing, to escape this danger.

"In the complex character of the population, we may see another ground for the exercise of prudence and caution. An adaptation of the formularies and system of the Church to the feelings and requirements of any one element may prove very unsuitable and mischievous in the instance of another.

"In the national jealousies, too, which usually prevail in a centre of resort such as this—one owing its independence to the forbearance of its more powerful neighbours—we have reason for care and circumspection."

Though the principles of Christian forbearance thus laid down have been adopted in practice as far as human infirmity would permit, yet the dangers foreseen have not been wholly evaded. The death of the King, in 1863, was followed by an outburst of most malignant writing in the Congregationalist organs, English and native, in Honolulu. To the credit of the more respected of the American missionaries and the French Romanists, it met with their strong reprobation. Still the assertion, dinned into the ears of the people week after week, that the Mission was all a scheme on the part of England to annex the Islands, and obtain more national influence in the Pacific, absurd as it was, had undoubtedly an evil effect. The most unscrupulous statements were circulated, to the effect that it was only intended to be a temporary measure, and that at any time it might withdraw, and leave those who united themselves with the Church "as sheep without a shepherd." So late as the beginning of last year, it was printed in the "Honolulu Advertiser," one of the organs referred to—of course without a shadow of foundation—that "the Society for Propagating the Gospel had, by a majority of nine to three, refused to give the Mission any further assistance," the authority being a statement to that effect made at a Congregationalist missionary meeting in the United States. Other assertions, intended to injure the influence of the Church, have been referred to in a previous chapter.

In the spring of 1867, the captain of a small American gunboat then in the harbour, at a gathering of American missionaries, held in their chief place of worship at Honolulu, thought it consistent with his profession to utter a tirade against England, and denounce the Bishop and clergy, contrasting the policy of England towards the natives in New Zealand with that of the United States towards the Hawaiians. To this and other similar attacks made from time to time on the members of the Mission, it has been their wont to make no reply, but, leaving it to others to defend them, rather to live down such abuse by the quiet and unobtrusive discharge of their duties.

It is fair to the American Government to say that its transactions with the Hawaiian kingdom have ever been conducted with honour, justice and consideration. The mischief arises from a small faction (what would in the United States be called ultra-Radical), living at Honolulu. From the bulk of the American residents the King's Government and the Anglican Church have both met with sympathy and respect. But the insolence that His Majesty has to endure from these intriguing politicians will be best illustrated by the fact, that, the Government at Washington having very properly ordered home the obnoxious gunboat, the offended captain wrote a letter to the Islands, strongly advocating their annexation to the United States, which was printed in the opposition journal, and circulated over the land!

When, in 1865, the House of American Bishops, by a resolution, expressed their sympathy with the Hawaiian Church, and admitted its chief pastor present among them as an honorary member of their House—an earnest of that unity, two years later, to be illustrated at Lambeth—the anger of the Puritan press of the United States knew no bounds. Articles were written in its principal organs, retailing all the malignant abuse that had reached them from the enemies of the Anglo-Hawaiian Church at Honolulu. The following, from the New York " Round Table," is a specimen. But for its mischievous intent, it might be amusing :—

"This British saint [the Bishop], under the genial tropical skies, quickly expands into a diplomatist; and under the soft, velvety glove of mellifluous religious rites, is the hard, clammy hand of Britain feeling for a naval station in the centre of the great tranquil sea. The Bishop has not slept at his post. Temporarily, at least, American influence is dead. We believe every dollar given to the Bishop strengthens the influence of a country that deceived a people in rebellion by promising aid, and insulted a nation by shielding piracy with international law."

Appeals such as this to the national susceptibilities greatly impeded the efforts that were made at the time to obtain funds in the United States. Nothing, however, could exceed the kindness of the President and Mr. Seward to the Bishop, under all the vituperation which he had to undergo, while both treated the charges of his being a political intriguer with the ridicule and contempt[1] they deserved. Bishop Kip, too, of San Francisco, wrote, in vindication of English Episcopacy in Hawaii, a letter which was deemed conclusive[2].

From a diplomatic correspondence published lately in the "Honolulu Gazette," it appears that even the visit of good Queen Emma to England, the pious and benevolent objects of which were above all suspicion, formed the subject of earnest representations to Washington on the part of the Rev. Rufus Anderson, Secretary of the American Congregationalist Board of Missions, who pointed out to Mr. Seward the political dangers to the United States that such contact of the humble Royalty of Hawaii with the intriguing Court of Great Britain might be expected to occasion.

---

[1] The "Boston Daily Advertiser," one of the most respectable journals in the country, said, in 1866, "We do not *insinuate*—we charge that this Mission is a part of a long-standing intrigue to make British influence paramount in a group of Islands which, politically, are the key which will hereafter control the Pacific."

Such writing as this must tell upon the American support of the Anglo-Hawaiian Church. "We trust," says the same journal, "that, in considering this subject, no member of the Episcopal Church of America will forget he still remains a citizen of the United States, and that he is to guard against any blow aimed at her influence or honour." All this was subsequent to the action of the House of American Bishops, a few months before. Nothing could be warmer than *their* sympathy, and that of the Board of Missions.

[2] Vide Appendix.

Nor would any thing satisfy this sensitive divine until despatches had been exchanged on the subject between Mr. Seward and the American minister in London!

It is obvious that the anticipations of the Farewell Sermon in Westminster Abbey, as to the kind of difficulties which would have to be met, have been more than realized. No forbearance, no courtesies, nothing can apparently mitigate the jealousy — if it would not be more correct to say the affectation of jealousy—that has been evoked. The absence of the Bishop in England to obtain funds, the unfinished state of the chancel, every needful change in the staff of labourers, are referred to as showing that the Anglican Church has no solid support, and will most likely be "withdrawn speedily from the Islands." Assurances from the clergy in private and public, letters from England, the arrival of stone-work for the cathedral, are all in vain as refutations of these assertions.

Yet, amid the calumny and persecution [3] to which the Anglo-Hawaiian Church and its royal supporters have had to submit, and which has certainly checked its growth, and retarded the *local* resources of a

---

[3] Many cases could be named of parents being threatened with social excommunication, and loss of employment, if they sent their children to the English schools or attended the Church.

pecuniary kind which it had a right to expect, it has more than held its own. So late as last February, a leading native wrote thus :—

"The Church is growing rapidly in the outside districts, such as Kona, Wailuku, and Lahaina. The local judge on Molokai, who is a member of our Church, states that there is a nice opening on that island; and, as the King lives a good deal there, a resident clergyman would not be out of the way. We want such men as ——, who are getting very popular with the natives."

There is much involved in a clergyman's "getting popular" when labouring among any of the Polynesian races. On the first start of every Mission of the Church, very much depends upon the acceptability and personal influence of the individuals composing its staff, as to how far or not it meets with success. Indeed, that a missionary should be "successful," it is almost essential that he should be "popular." Such men are not always forthcoming. There may be zeal, ability, energy, self-denial; but without untiring patience, tact and good temper, all will be in vain. The natives are not slow in finding out, too, whether a man is come to devote himself, in a true missionary spirit, to their welfare and improvement; to live permanently, as well as labour among them, or only for a few years, as a stepping-stone to something else. The harm done by men leaving a Mission after a few years' work, however efficient it may have been, exceeds the benefit of their services. The difficulty of the language has been, perhaps, just surmounted when the post is abandoned, and a successor has to be found, who has again to go through the same process and encounter the same difficulties. Thus, no *way* is made; while the unhinging of the native mind, the constantly having to begin afresh, the inevitable result—a loss of all confidence, are most mischievous.

The Roman Catholics have an advantage in this respect in their foreign missionary work. A priest goes out to live and die among his flock. He *never* thinks of returning to his native land, except in his old age; and very rarely even then.

And if stability in its *personnel* is requisite to the success of a Mission, not less so is it in the matter of pecuniary resources. For a native population to know that their chief pastor is absent in order to procure the means of maintaining his work among them—that it is implied in his very office, that he should, every few years, leave them, "as sheep without a shepherd," to stimulate the flagging zeal of his fellow-Churchmen at home by descriptions of his work and reports of his success—must be every way a sad discovery for them to make. It may be doubted how far any Church can properly be said to be a Missionary Church at all, that imposes this duty upon those who hold her Divine Commission to go among the heathen. After being thirty years in the Sandwich Islands, the French Vicar Apostolic is supplied with ample funds from the French branch of the Propaganda at Lyons, not only so as to maintain all his priests and nuns, but to erect picturesque neat stone churches at all the chief places. In a letter dated April 29th this year, Mr. Whipple, of Wailuku, states that "the Romanists have just begun to build one there, where Anglicans have only a wooden school-church; and that it is to cost $6000, all furnished to the Vicar Apostolic from his supporters at home."

It may well be asked whether, with better-marshalled forces, more certain supplies of money, a machinery for its disposal simpler and more centralized, Rome can fail to have the advantage in her foreign missionary work, notwithstanding our purer

Faith, and our more attractive, because more intelligible, ritual.

On the whole, it may be said that the future vigour and development of the Church in Hawaii depend very much, and will do so for some years to come, upon external support. Surely, considering the years that England suffered these Islands to remain unblest with the light of Christianity—years during which the Anglo-Saxon race was introducing into them forms of evil, physical as well as moral, before unknown—that support ought by her to be cheerfully and ungrudgingly given.

VII.

SKETCH OF THE ISLANDS AND PEOPLE, COMMERCE,
SOCIAL CONDITION, ETC.

THE maritime importance of the Hawaiian Archipelago depends mainly on its geographical position. Running diagonally from N.W. to S.E. over the greater part of 300 miles, a segment of a parallel of latitude through its centre would, at its extremities, touch Southern China on the west, and Central Mexico on the east. Thus it furnishes a place of refreshment and rest for vessels engaged in the whaling and carrying trades of the Pacific, as well as for ships of war. Last year (1867) the following were the entries at the port of Honolulu :—

    Whalers 87
    Merchantmen 109
    National vessels . . . 9

The tonnage of the merchant ships amounted to

42,962, of which 11,495 was British, the rest of other nations.

When the line of steamers between San Francisco and Japan commenced running, it was intended that they should coal at Honolulu on their way. Accordingly, the Government deepened the harbour, and extended the wharf seawards, that steamers drawing upwards of twenty feet of water might enter. Subsequently the Company preferred to make the great circle course, and carry coal for the whole voyage. So far, the experiment seems to have failed. The run is seldom, if ever, made in the time proposed —twenty-two days. It has been in some instances so long as thirty days; and the latest advices state that the steamers will probably touch at Honolulu, after all. More room will be available for freight; the exhaustion of fuel before the completion of the voyage will be avoided; and thus the passage, though in mileage longer, will be more certain and more profitable. If, as sometimes suggested, a British line of steamers should hereafter run from Panama to China, they cannot fail to call at Honolulu. The communication between the Islands and San Francisco is at present maintained by sailing barques, running very irregularly, and a monthly steamer.

To supply the wants of the merchants and whaling vessels, and of the natives and foreign residents, goods, chiefly manufactured, were imported last year to the amount of $1,899,193, or 379,200*l.*, nearly one-half of this being in the items of articles of clothing, hardware, implements, and textile fabrics. There is a custom-house, and the revenue of the kingdom is raised by an *ad valorem* duty of 10 per cent. on all imports.

In the session of this year's Legislature, assembled at Honolulu, a measure has been discussed for raising a part of the revenue by direct taxation, in order that, should a reciprocity treaty be negotiated, as the Government desires, with the United States for the free interchange of trade, the consequent falling off in the customs may be made good by other resources.

But it may be asked, What is the productive industry of these Islands? what can they *export?* The answers to these questions must be introduced with a few words as to their physical geography.

There can be no doubt that the whole archipelago has been uplifted from the bed of the ocean by volcanic pressure. Niihau and Kauai are the oldest; Oahu and Maui stand next in antiquity; Hawaii being the only member of the group now troubled with volcanic action [1].

It is interesting to observe how the display of active volcanic influence has retreated from the N.W. to the S.E. through the Islands generally, and how it still appears to be doing so in Hawaii now. Symptoms have been found which prove the uplifting process to be still silently going on in the Hawaiian Islands, while those in the South Pacific seem rather to belong to the plane of submersion.

Situated only just within the limit of the northern tropic, and in the region of the N.E. trades, which blow the greater part of the year, and convey the ocean vapours, condensed into clouds, over the mountains and table-lands, then to fall in fertilizing showers—the country enjoys a luxuriant and delicious climate. The average annual temperature is 77° F., with only a few degrees' variation above and below. But the local climates are varied, depending on aspect and elevation. At Waimea, on a plateau about 4000 feet above the sea-level, in the north of Hawaii, a fire in your bed-room is a necessity. On the other hand, the houses at Honolulu and many other places are built without chimneys, no fires being needed at any

[1] See Appendix.

period of the year. Generally speaking, there is more rain on the windward than the leeward sides of the Islands. Hence the rich green hues of the eastern slopes of Hawaii, covered with verdure and cultivation, contrast strongly with the bare and arid look of the coast on the greater part of the western side.

There is no tropical wet season, in the ordinary sense of the term—that is, at the summer epoch. On the contrary, the wettest part of the year is when the sun's vertical is the furthest removed from the northern tropic—viz., in December and January. Then abundant rain falls, storms of great violence, called *Konas*, suddenly arise, and the inter-island navigation has to be suspended.

With a climate so genial, something between temperate and tropical, and a soil formed from the *débris* of volcanic rock, agriculture may be expected to flourish.

Niihau is a sheep farm, 15 miles long by about 3. It is in the occupation of a Scotch family, who migrated hither from Canterbury, New Zealand. They are large exporters of wool.

In Kauai are cattle ranches, sheep-farms, and the largest sugar plantation in the kingdom, formerly belonging to the late Robert Wyllie, Esq. Oahu, 50 miles long by an average width of 10 to 15 miles, possesses two large tracts of land, one in the N.W. corner, the other on the N.E. slope, on which thousands of cattle and sheep are fed. The former is the property of Mr. R. Moffitt, an Irish gentleman, who has greatly improved the island stock by crossing it with the best English breeds. He has Herefords and Devons among his cattle, and his sheep are a cross between the Southdown and the Merino. There are sugar plantations in Oahu, and lately cotton has been grown there successfully. Maui divided by an isthmus of sand into East and West is, by eminence, the sugar-growing island; while the slopes of the wonderful extinct crater Haleokala ("house of the sun"), 20 miles in the circumference of the upper rim, and 10,000 feet high, furnish a valuable pasturage.

The central part of Hawaii, which is nearly 90 miles from N. to S., is a great desert of lava of every known kind. It is only the northern plain, the eastern slope, and some portions of the south and west, which are productive, and where are to be found sugar estates, and cattle ranches, and sheep runs equal to any in the world. Mauna Kea, an extinct volcano, 13,000 feet high, covered with perpetual snow, has hundreds of wild cattle pasturing on its slopes.

In this island is found *pulu*, a fibrous silky material, which grows out of the top of the trunk of a certain tree-fern. It is collected at certain periods and exported to America, where it is much used to stuff mattresses with. No where on the same area in extent is so great a variety of ferns to be found as in this island.

Native labour is not adequate to the demand, and some thousands of coolies from China have been introduced to work on the sugar estates. The planters are British, American, or German, as are also the mercantile houses in Honolulu which conduct the business of the country.

The following were the chief exports, in lbs., for 1867:—

Sugar	17,127,187—
	that is, about 700 tons monthly.
Rice	441,750
Coffee	127,546
Pulu	203,958
Wool	409,471
Hides	304,095
Molasses	544,994 gals.
&c.,	&c.

Money commands generally about 1 per cent.

interest per month, or 12 per cent. per annum. Skilled labour, as that of mechanics, carpenters, and masons, from 10s. to 15s. a day. Labourers on plantations secure little more than 1s. as their daily wages. Domestic service is not suited to the native ideas; but they work well as cultivators of the soil.

The food of the Hawaiian people is of a very simple kind. It is made from a root called the *kalo* (taro) (*arum esculentum*), grown under water, which, after being cooked in the ground and reduced to meal, is mixed with water and made into a paste, called *poi*. It is then put into calabashes, and allowed slightly to ferment, when it is eaten, usually with salt fish as a relish. There can be no doubt it is a highly nutritious and healthy food.

The native dwellings are made sometimes of an indigenous grass and the pandanus leaf, sometimes of wood, very rarely of stone. They usually consist of one room separated into two compartments by curtains of *kapa*, the native cloth formed from the inner bark of the *morus papyrifera*, which, having been reduced to a pulp, and then pressed, is dried in the sun. It is rarely, in the outlying districts at least, that they contain any provision for the separation of the sexes, or for maintaining the decencies of life.

Except on Sundays and *fête* days, the Hawaiian dress is of the most scant kind. The women wear a loose gown of calico hanging from the shoulders, not "gathered in" at the waist; the men, when *kalo*-planting or doing other manual labour, often have nothing on in the way of clothing, except a belt round their loins, called the *malo*. There can be no doubt that the sudden change which they are wont to make, from the heavy finery of European dress one day to this cooler costume another, greatly injures their constitutions, and causes many deaths. They have little faith in European remedies, preferring their own herb-medicines, which they often administer with incantations and other heathen rites. One of them is the *awa* plant—in moderation, proved to be a valuable purifier of the blood; but when used in excess, as a narcotic, most injurious. The Government is obliged to restrict its sale. It is to the credit of the Hawaiians, that as a nation they are alive to the mischief occasioned by stimulating drinks. For many years they have maintained an embargo on the sale of all such liquors to the native population; and its violation entails fine or imprisonment on the offender. The repeal of this law has been often proposed in the Legislature, only to be rejected. Still, it must be confessed that there is at all times more or less secret drinking. The prickly pear, the root called the *ki*, and other vegetables, are widely used for distillation, and yield liquors of a very noxious character. It can hardly be said, however, that drinking is the vice which is destroying the population. All who have studied the subject are agreed that its frightful decrease of late years has been due rather to licentiousness and prostitution. The Government was bound to recognize the existence of these evils, and not shrink from the task of grappling with them. Accordingly, an Act was passed, in 1859, called " An Act to mitigate," &c.—very much of the same nature as that which has been adopted with success in the arsenals and navy ports of Great Britain for the protection of the sailors and soldiers resorting thither. Its result has been most beneficial in stemming the progress of disease, and diminishing immorality.

There is a complete system of common schools supported by the State, where every native child has the opportunity of learning to read, write, and cipher in his own tongue. Of course, there is nothing of a literature in the Hawaiian language for them to be acquainted with; but they have the Bible, Prayer Book, and other religious works, a few books on secular subjects, and their native newspapers. There are two weekly ones in Honolulu, one supporting the Government, and the other the Opposition, in which, however, articles on other than political topics are to be found. Parents are *compelled* to send their children to these or the English schools, under penalty of the law. They are, of course, secular schools, though the Bible is read, without note or comment. Government English day-schools, on the other hand—which of late have so much increased in number—are on the denominational principle, with, however, what may be termed "a conscience clause." For example: at Lahaina the Government English school is in the hands of the Ven. Archdeacon Mason. The great majority of the boys, upwards of eighty, attend the daily service. But the children of Roman Catholics do not present themselves at school until Matins are ended.

Family boarding-schools for girls come under a third category. No such exemptions on the grounds of "conscience" are required in them as a condition of Government support. The reason is, that each "denomination" can provide such schools for its own members, and they are only *in part* sustained by a system of capitation grants paid for results, and in proportion to the length of training in such schools; whereas there is only one Government day-school for teaching English in each island, and it is *wholly* supported by the State.

Life and property in the Hawaiian Islands are as secure as in any part of the civilized world. The traveller who turns into a native house in the wildest and most remote parts even of Hawaii, is sure to meet with a kind and hospitable reception. There is an excellent system of roads, which are carried, sometimes with considerable engineering skill, over mountains and down *palis*[2]. The kingdom is organized into districts for the administration of justice, and there is an efficient police.

The highest or Supreme Court of the realm consists of three judges. One is a Hawaiian, another an American, the third was a British lawyer, who died last year; his successor has not yet been appointed. The maritime position of the kingdom, giving rise to numerous difficult Admiralty cases, requires, above all things, an efficient judiciary.

The King governs by a Cabinet (in which he usually sits himself, taking part in their deliberations), containing a Minister of the Interior, a Minister of

---

[2] *Pali* is the native word for precipice.

Foreign Affairs, a Minister of Finance, an Attorney-General. These gentlemen, usually intelligent foreigners of character, sit *ex officio* in the Legislative Chamber.

That chamber, which makes the laws, subject to the King's approval, is of a composite character, having in it nobles and chiefs, "not more than twenty," and about forty representatives, who must have in real estate 100*l.*, or have an income of 50*l.*, derived from property or some lawful occupation, and be able to read and write. Voters must be possessed of real estate to the amount of 30*l.*, or be able to show an income of 15*l.* yearly derived from property or honest wages. There is also a Privy Council of State, consisting of thirty members.

Each island has its Viceroy. The one who presides over the Island of Hawaii is the King's half-sister, Keelikolani, known better by the title of "*Governess* of Hawaii."

If the King has no direct heirs, he may nominate his successor, subject to the approval of his House of Nobles. But should he die without having made such nomination, the Legislative Chamber is convoked by the Cabinet, who are, *pro tempore*, regents; and this chamber then elects one of the high chiefs to be the founder of a new royal *stirps*.

The present Constitution was the free gift of his present Hawaiian Majesty to his people, in 1864. There can be no doubt, that under its simple and stringent provisions much has been done for the moral and social advancement of the Hawaiian race. The last census proves, however, that much remains yet to be done in this direction. The total population has decreased to 62,959 in 1867, from 69,700 in 1860; and of these 4194 are foreigners.

The family schools for girls that have been established must, in a few years, have an influence in arresting this fearful diminution. At least, it is the duty of all in whom a spark of "the enthusiasm of humanity" exists, to do what they can to preserve from perishing off the face of the earth, a race endued with so many noble and loving traits as the Hawaiian.

APPENDIX.

P. 14.

The Bishop of California's Letter.

"THE HAWAIIAN EPISCOPATE.

" To the Editor of the ' Pacific Churchman ' :—

" For five years past, Mr. Editor, the secular press, and a part of that called ' the religious,' have rung with misrepresentations about the appointment, by the English Church, of Dr. Staley as Bishop of Honolulu. It was represented to be entirely a political move, intended to strengthen English influence at the Sandwich Islands. The whole *charge*, indeed, was thus summed up in a sentence in your last number :—

" ' The Episcopal Mission to those Islands originated in a " political object on the part of the English Government," and Bishop Staley was sent out as " a political Missionary." '

" Now, as I probably had more to do than any one in this country with the origin of this arrangement, it is but proper that I should explain. Perhaps I should have done so before; but I have held back from a disinclination to speak personally on this matter. I think, however, that a plain statement of the whole affair will be sufficient to put at rest for ever the absurd stories which have been circulated. I do it, therefore, over my own name.

"Previous to 1860, I had received repeated applications from the Islands to send a clergyman of our Church. The late Hon. W. C. Wyllie, Minister of Foreign Relations, several times wrote to me on the subject. Unfortunately, we had no clergy to spare, there not being half enough for the work of our own Diocese. I applied to members both of the Domestic and Foreign Committees in New York, but received no encouragement. It was clearly not within the sphere of action of the Domestic Committee, while the late Rev. Dr. Turner wrote to me, on the part of the Foreign Committee, that 'not considering the Sandwich Islands a heathen land, it was not within their field.'

"In the summer of 1860 I went to England. During the previous spring, Mr. Wyllie (knowing my intention) again wrote to me, by direction of the late King, requesting me to make an arrangement for them in England, to which Church he had already, I believe, applied. A number of letters on the subject passed, mine being submitted to the King, and the answer dictated by him to Mr. Wyllie. Hopeless of obtaining any clergy from our own country to establish the Church in Hawaii, I agreed to further that object in England.

"Accordingly, when in London, in July, 1860, I brought the matter before the Bishops of Oxford and London, both of whom entered heartily into it. I particularly remember one evening at Fulham Palace, when I showed Mr. Wyllie's letters to the Bishop of London, and we went fully into the matter. It was agreed that it should be *a joint Mission*—that two or three clergy should be sent out by the Church of England, and the same number by the American Church, when practicable. The *animus* of the whole affair was shown in a single remark made to me on this occasion by the Bishop of London: 'I am happy,' said he, 'that the application for this Mission comes from an American Bishop, so that it cannot be said that the Church of England is obtruding itself on the Islands.' This single remark settles the whole point at issue which has since been made by the opponents of the Mission.

"A public meeting, to be presided over by the Bishop of Oxford, was then called, and I was requested to be present to make necessary explanations. As I had an engagement in the country, which prevented my being there, I wrote a long letter to the Bishop of Oxford, giving all the statements which I had verbally made to him and the Bishop of London. When I next met him, he told me that 'my letter was read at the meeting, and then placed on file, to show at any future time their reasons for this action.'

"I would mention also that the Bishop of New York, who was then in England, being consulted, gave his cordial approbation to the measure.

"The application which I made was only with reference to sending some clergy to Honolulu. The plan was afterwards expanded to embrace sending a Bishop also as head of the Mission, until it assumed its present form, wisely presenting the Church in its entireness.

"Now, Mr. Editor, this is a simple statement of the whole matter; and you will see how perfectly absurd is the charge of 'English influence' and 'English politics.' The appeal was not made to England until after it had been made in vain to our own Church. The application to the English Bishops was made by me, to supply what I knew to be a religious want at the Islands. With any present controversies about the Hawaiian Church I have nothing to do, and have no occasion now to make any reference to them; but it must be very evident, that a measure inaugurated *at the request of an American Bishop* was not intended to 'increase English influence' in the Islands.

"I make this statement, therefore, as a mere historical matter, and in justice to the Church of England and the Bishop of Honolulu.

"WM. INGRAHAM KIP,
"Bishop of California.

"SAN FRANCISCO,
"*Sept.* 21*st*, 1866."

P. 53.

Copy of the Article of the Constitution relating to Qualification of Members of the Legislature and of Voters.

"ARTICLE 61. No person shall be eligible for a Representative of the People who is insane or an idiot; nor, unless he be a male subject of the Kingdom, who shall have arrived at the full age of Twenty-one years—who shall know how to read and write—who shall understand accounts—and shall have been domiciled in the Kingdom for at least three years, the last of which shall be the year immediately preceding his election; and who shall own Real Estate, within the Kingdom, of a clear value, over and above all incumbrances, of at least Five Hundred Dollars; or who shall have an annual income of at least Two Hundred and Fifty Dollars, derived from any property, or some lawful employment.

"ARTICLE 62. Every male subject of the Kingdom who shall have paid his taxes, who shall have attained the age of Twenty years, and shall have been domiciled in the Kingdom for one year immediately preceding the election, and shall be possessed of Real Property in this Kingdom to the value, over and above all incumbrances, of One Hundred and Fifty Dollars—or of a Leasehold property on which the rent is Twenty-five Dollars per year, or of an income of not less than Seventy-five Dollars per year, derived from any property or some lawful employment, and shall know how to read and write, if born since the year 1840, and shall have caused his name to be entered on the list of voters of his District as may be provided by law, —shall be entitled to one vote for the Representative or Representatives of that District. *Provided, however,* that no insane or idiotic person, nor any person who shall have been convicted of any infamous crime within this Kingdom, unless he shall have been pardoned by the King, and by the terms of such pardon have been restored to all the rights of a subject, shall be allowed to vote."

P. 54.

Queen Emma's Visit.

Her Majesty left Honolulu on May 6th, 1865, in H.B.M. ship "Clio," arriving in London on July the 14th. She was obliged to leave England for the winter, and only remained a short time the following year on her way back to the Islands.

It is needless to remark on the interest which she inspired, and the kindly welcome which she everywhere met with.

About 6000*l*. was contributed, during her brief visit, to the Cathedral Fund and other objects connected with the spiritual and educational work of the Mission.

APPENDIX.

P. 58.

The Sisters of Mercy, in 1864, on their way to Southampton to embark, halted at Hursley, and were there kindly received by Mr. Keble. He preached and celebrated with them the Holy Communion during their stay. The following extract from his Sermon proves the deep interest which he felt in their work, and how well he understood it :—

"You will have, please God, many remembering you here—many prayers earnestly and affectionately said—often by those who would wish to follow you, if God's providence so pointed their way. Many waiting for news of your work, as men wait for letters and reports of friends and kinsmen out in the Queen's service; and especially those connected with penitentiary work, who dwell in houses of the highest kind of mercy; for your work, if I rightly understand, will probably, in an especial manner, correspond with theirs—to cure or assuage, but rather, by God's blessing, to prevent the sin and misery which employs their charity here,—teaching the young persons with whom God may entrust you to know their high calling and the glory and bliss of purity.

"There are encouragements here, and surely we may say in thankfulness that there are great encouragements there. It has pleased Him to bring that to pass in Hawaii which He hath wrought in divers countries on which He was looking with an eye of compassion: in our own, as you know, for one. The conversion of England began in some sort from a Queen; and in Hawaii He has raised up a Queen, of whom I will only say thus much—taking it from a letter which I received yesterday from the Bishop of Honolulu himself:—' She seeks her consolation' (for you know that within a short time she has had to part from her only child first, and then from her husband)—' She seeks her consolation in God, and in furthering the work of His Church, and is ever at the side of the sick and dying.' Surely we are not wrong in accepting this as a happy token of what is to come.

"In this and in many other respects, I doubt not your experiencing the truth of that other proverb, which our Lord uttered at the well by Sichem for the encouragement of His Missionaries: 'One soweth, and another reapeth.' Your chosen field is far from being altogether wild and rough: others have been labouring there; and you, the first Mission Sisters whom the English Church will [have sent out] will now have to enter on the fruit of their labours. Be it more or less, it will be an earnest of the Holy Spirit working in the hearts [of the people], to prepare them for the further help which He has disposed you to offer them.

"Of this men see and hear; but He who has promised to be with us has deep mysterious ways—ways of working in silence to bring about the good which

He is providing for those whom He sees fit for His kingdom; and it becomes us humbly to brace up our faith and hope by meditating sometimes on those His unrevealed means of grace. Who knows but at this very time, somewhere in the country to which our thoughts are being drawn, tender women—mothers, wives, and sisters, in temptation, or in trouble for others who are so—may be praying for just such help as you by His grace will bring to them. God grant that there may be many such prayers—that ours may be worthy to meet them, as it were, in the air, and that both may go up as sweet incense for a memorial before God. Who knows but that there may be some 'woman of Samaria,' the course of whose life may be receiving such a turn from God's providence, even in the very sins which He permits but overrules, that by and by she may come, as it were by accident, to the place where some of you will be, and bring a heart ready to hear the words of love and truth which you will say? O my dear brothers and sisters, were it but one soul won in this or any other way to faith in Christ and eternal life, how great, how glorious, how unspeakably sweet and blessed the portion of him or her whom God shall so employ! Think of the Apostle's saying, 'That I may present you as a chaste virgin to Christ.' And think, each one of you, what it must be to have the witness of the Lord Himself from His throne of glory, 'Thou, even thou, hast been My instrument in bringing this sinner to penitence and perfection; well done, good and faithful servant;

do thou—with him or her whom thou hast brought to Me—enter into the joy of thy Lord.'

"We know not what that 'joy' will be; but thus much we know, that it will in part be the same joy which is felt in heaven, in the presence of the angels of God, over one sinner that repenteth—the same joy of which He spake, when He promised His true Missionaries not only wages in this world,—the comfort of His loving presence and the delight of working for Him only,—but fruit gathered unto life eternal; when 'He that soweth'—that is the Son of man himself— 'and he that reapeth,' shall 'rejoice together.'

"God only knows which of us all will persevere and win that crown; but we and you may humbly thank Him and take courage from the very lessons providentially read to-day. Our cause cannot fail, for it is written, 'The earth shall be filled with the knowledge of the glory of the Lord, as the waters cover the sea' (Hab. ii. 14). Our strength will be proportioned to our need; for we have Him with us who twice fed thousands with a basketful of bread and fish (Matt. xv. 32), who has built a home on the rock for such as take up His cross. We hear His prophet resolving, that if all seem failing on earth, he will 'rejoice in the Lord,' he will 'joy in the God of his salvation' (Hab. iii. 18). And, what seems to come very near to you, my sisters, we have many of the women, S. Paul's fellow-labourers, the like of those concerning whom he says, 'Their names are in the book of life,' —we have them reckoned up one by one, with most affectionate blessings sent from a far land and acknowledgments of labour—'much labour'—done 'in the Lord' (Rom. xvi.).

"And He has sealed all these good words to us by permitting us to partake of His blessed Sacrifice and Sacrament.

"Is it not, we may humbly think, as if we heard His voice saying, 'Go forth in the strength of the Lord God'—only have no selfish ends—'make mention of His righteousness only.'?"

P. 68.

The late Volcanic Eruption.

The celebrated pit crater Kilauea lies on a table-land, instead of forming the summit of a mountain. The fiery lake in this crater is always more or less active. But it was Mauna Loa (on whose eastern flank, nearer the sea, Kilauea is situated) that so recently burst forth, opening a new crater, and sending a stream of burning lava in a S.S.W. direction into the sea[1], destroying life and property to a frightful extent, and converting some of the fairest portions of southern Hawaii into a desert of cinders and mud. The first symptom was an earthquake, ten days before the flow began, followed by repeated shocks at longer or

---

[1] See Map.

shorter intervals. In *four* days 300 of these earthquakes occurred, of which, however, the other islands were scarcely sensible. The Rev. C. G. Williamson, at Kona, carefully registered these 300 shocks in his journal, with the direction, duration, and general character of each,—a valuable contribution to those who study the branch of geology bearing on volcanic agency. One of the most terrible features in this convulsion of nature was a huge tidal wave on the S.E. coast, which rose to the tops of the cocoa-nut trees, and rushed inland, prostrating all before it in one common ruin.

Queen Emma at once opened a subscription-list for the sufferers, whom the King went in person to relieve with supplies of food and clothing, and remove to a place of security.

P. 91.

S. Andrew's Cathedral.

The general character of the structure will be inferred from the engraving given of the elevation in this volume. The following is a description, taken from the " Building News " of April 10, 1868, of the portion now in hand :—

" The length of the choir from the first step to the

outside of the apse columns, we may observe, is 45 feet. It has been the object of the architects to convey the cathedral idea more by the general plan and arrangement of the building than by any grandeur of design or physical magnitude. The local deficiency of building materials made it specially necessary to study simplicity in its details, for there were only two courses open—either to send out the masons' work complete from England, or to build the whole of rough stone, plastered inside and out. A design embodying the latter idea was, as will be remembered, at first proposed, highly decorated with colour in the interior; but the other expedient was considered to be the best, and has been acted on. The choir has three bays, with a polygonal apse of five arches, the processional path being continued all round it, with coupled windows in each bay. The columns of the arcade are cylindrical, with carved capitals, and the arches have two orders of simple mouldings. Above them runs a string of ornamental terra cotta under the sills of the clerestory windows. In each bay of the clerestory are two lancet lights with coupled shafts; the bays of the apse have one light. The bays are divided by shafts resting on corbels above the arcade caps. These shafts run up to the level of the springing of the clerestory windows, at which level spring also the arched ribs of the roof. The whole of the roof is of timber, and boarded and panelled between the trusses, and is intended to be decorated with colour. For the ordinary walling black basalt and reef-stone (cut from the reefs by the native prisoners) is used. The natives thoroughly understand and can execute this sort of walling satisfactorily; but skilled masons' labour is very expensive, as much as five or six dollars a day being asked. Oregon timber and American pine are used for the roofs, which are covered with tiles. The windows of the clerestory will be filled with coloured glass; but the aisle windows will have movable glazed sashes, and inside Venetian shutters. The stone used for the arcades and windows is Ketton, white Mansfield, and Doulting. There will be two rows of stalls, six in number, on each side, the Dean and Precentor's stalls being respectively at the west end of the north and south blocks, and the Chancellor and Treasurer's stalls at the eastern end. The Bishop's throne will be on the south side, eastward of the stalls. The altar is raised seven steps above the nave level, and will have over it a lofty baldachin of metal work. A low iron screen is to stand in the western arch; and there will also be iron grilles in all the side and apse arches, with gates opening into the processional path."

P. 96.

Origin of the Polynesian Race.

There seems to be evidence that the Arian, or Sanscrit-speaking, race descended from the north-west of Hindostan thousands of years ago, and subdued the original Turanian inhabitants.

Many of these would be forced into the Archipelago, to the S.E. of Asia, driving the black aborigines into the interior of some of the islands and peninsulas, and entirely expelling them from others. (What is called Melanesia consists of islands where the race with black skins and woolly crispy hair still remain.) In this way, the tide of Turanian emigration swept through Malayisia into the islands which lie South and North of the Equator over about two-thirds of the Pacific, and known as "Polynesia." The languages spoken throughout these groups are Turanian, that is, in an agglutinative stage, distinguished by the merely mechanical union of their particles, which are glued to the root, as it were, instead of growing out of it. Take the verb *aloha*, "love." The particle *ke*, before, and *nei*, after, express *present* action. *Ke* aloha *nei* = do love. Hawaiian is a language of particles. The languages of East Malayisia, especially of the Moluccas, approach nearest of any of the Turanian groups to those of Polynesia. And it is probable that these would be the starting points of the first Polynesian emigrants.

ADDENDA.

Note 1, p. 100.

One of the rich pasture grasses is that known as the *menenia*, introduced from Asia. It runs along the ground, sending shoots into the soil, and covering the area on which it is planted with great rapidity. The wires which it forms by this horizontal growth are often four and five feet long. It makes a sweet and nutritious hay, and is cut, not with the scythe, but the sickle.

Note 2.

The shield, with its device, on the cover and title-page of this volume, is a copy of a very beautiful banner lately worked for the diocese of Honolulu, and presented by an English lady.

The S. Andrew's Cross refers to the fact of the Church at Honolulu being dedicated to S. Andrew, the King having deceased on the festival of that Apostle.

Above it is the Hawaiian Crown, the symbolism of the whole being indicated by the legend " He lanakila ma ke kea," " Victory by the Cross."

✠

Note 3.

P.S.—The portrait of Queen Emma is not among those which have been selected for this publication, simply because it is now almost a household one in this country, or at least familiar to all who are likely to read a work on the enterprise of which she is the life and soul.

ERRATA.

Pages 20 and 29, *for* Mani *read* Maui
— 75 and 77, *for* Kalakana *read* Kalakaua
— 18, line 18, *for* T. B. Cantuar. *read* J. B. Cantuar.
— 23, — 4, *for* us *read* the Church
— 25, — 11, *for* independence of *read* independence by
— 75, — 5, *for* we *read* it is thought well to
— 79, — 20, *for* we may affirm *read* it may be truly affirmed
— 93, — 7, *before* exceeds *insert* almost
— 102, — 5, *for* mattresses *read* mattrasses
— 107, — 23, *for* their *read* its

LONDON:
GILBERT AND RIVINGTON, PRINTERS,
ST. JOHN'S SQUARE.